uncommon
youthelective

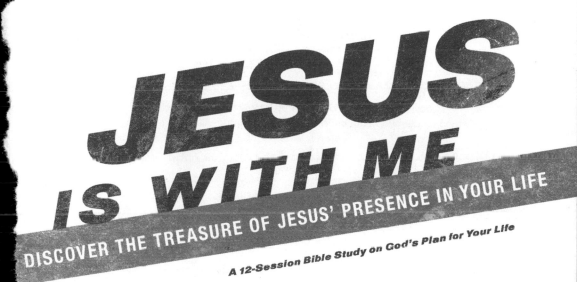

JESUS IS WITH ME

DISCOVER THE TREASURE OF JESUS' PRESENCE IN YOUR LIFE

A 12-Session Bible Study on God's Plan for Your Life

"Jesus Christ is the same yesterday
and today and forever."—Hebrews 13:8

Published by Gospel Light
Ventura, California, U.S.A.
www.gospellight.com
Printed in the U.S.A.

Text written by Christie Goeser and Elizabeth Wingate.

Library of Congress Cataloging-in-Publication Data
Jesus is with me : discover the treasure of Jesus' presence in your life.
pages cm
"Jesus Christ is the same yesterday and today and forever. Hebrews 13:8."
ISBN 978-0-8307-6524-9 (trade paper)
1. Christian life—Study and teaching. 2. Church work with teenagers.
3. Church group work. I. Gospel Light Publications (Firm)
BV4511.J47 2013
248.4071'2—dc23
2012051390

Rights for publishing this book outside the U.S.A. or in non-English languages are
administered by Gospel Light Worldwide, an international not-for-profit ministry.
For additional information, please visit www.glww.org, email info@glww.org, or write
to Gospel Light Worldwide, 1957 Eastman Avenue, Ventura, CA 93003, U.S.A.

To order copies of this book and other Gospel Light products in bulk quantities,
please contact us at 1-800-446-7735.

Contents

How to Use the
Jesus Is with Me
Group Study Guide

This Uncommon junior-high elective group study contains 12 sessions. Although this study can be used with your junior-high students alongside Gospel Light's Vacation Bible School program *SonWest Roundup*, it can also be used as a stand-alone study. The first five sessions complement the children's Vacation Bible School, while the remaining sessions can be used to make this into a 12-week study.

	VBS Session	Uncommon Big Idea
Session 1	Ultimate PLAN	God used Moses in His plan to rescue the Israelites, and He sent Jesus to fulfill His plan to rescue us.
Session 2	Ultimate POWER	God is the ultimate source of power, and He wants to use His power to help us.
Session 3	Ultimate RESCUE	God rescued the Israelites at Passover, and Jesus is the Passover Lamb who rescued us from sin and gives us eternal life.
Session 4	Ultimate TRUST	We can rely on God to take care of us.
Session 5	Ultimate LOVE	God wants us to follow His commandments, which were summed up by Jesus: love God and love each other.

This is your leader's guidebook for teaching your group. Electronic files (in PDF format) for each session's student handouts are available online at **www.gospellight.com/uncommon/jh_Jesus_is_with_me.zip**. The handouts include the "Reflect" section of each study, formatted for easy printing, in addition to any student worksheets for the session. You may print as many copies as you need for your group.

Each individual session begins with a brief overview of the big idea of the lesson, the aims of the session, the primary Bible verse, and additional verses that tie in to the topic being discussed. The 12 sessions are geared to be 45 to 90 minutes in length. If you are using this alongside the *SonWest Roundup* Vacation Bible School Program, you may want to incorporate the following elements into each session to round out your program (there are several *Uncommon* youth resources available from gospellight.com to help you with ideas):

1. Start your session by attending the *SonWest Roundup* opening assembly time.

2. Involve your students in making and sharing a snack.

3. Provide time for worship and singing. Talk to your VBS director about music available through the *SonWest Roundup* program.

4. Prepare a craft idea or creative activity that students can work on together or individually (group projects may include creating a mural, working on a service project, or making a video).

5. Include the "Reflect" section during your session to encourage your students to spend a little solo time with God.

6. Have a large-group game planned that incorporates the *SonWest Roundup* theme (again, your VBS director has a wealth of ideas available. You may also want to use *Uncommon Games & Icebreakers,* available from Gospel Light, for ideas).

OVERALL LESSON OBJECTIVE

Sometimes, it can seem as if we are living in the Wild West. Problems come our way that we don't know how to solve, and our situation feels completely out of control. We wonder if there is anyone out there to help us or if we will have to be "lone rangers" and figure out how to cope by ourselves. During such times, God wants us to know that He cares about what we are going through and that

He is always with us. He has promised to never leave us (see John 14:18), and He has given us examples throughout the Bible of how He directly intervened in people's lives to help them through tough times. One of these examples, which your group members will study, is the story of how God delivered the Israelites from Egypt.

SESSION COMPONENTS

Starter: Depend *on* Him
Depending on Jesus begins with us recognizing His presence in our lives. To that end, each lesson begins with an activity that will introduce your students to the main theme of the lesson and get them interacting with others in the group.

Message: Learn *from* Him
As we learn from God and His Word, we will better understand that Jesus is always with us, regardless of the situations we are facing. In this section, the group members will begin to explore the main Bible story for the session and see how God was always faithful to His people.

Dig: Live *for* Him
Once we understand the Bible's promises that Jesus is always with us, we can truly begin to live our lives for Him with confidence. To this end, in this section the group members will dig a bit deeper into the Bible and study other passages that illustrate the main theme of the session.

Apply: Move *to* Him
It's not enough to just know that Jesus is with us—we also need to take action and move to Him. This occurs when we purposefully pursue an ongoing fellowship with Him. Each session, therefore, ends with a specific step that students can take as they walk toward His will.

Reflect: Be *with* Him
We learn to trust that Jesus will always be with us when we spend time with Him. These short devotions are for the students to reflect on and answer during the week. You can make copies of these pages and distribute them to your class, or you can download and print them from **www.gospellight.com/ uncommon/jh_Jesus_is_with_me.zip.**

ULTIMATE PLAN

THE BIG IDEA

God used Moses in His plan to rescue the Israelites, and He sent Jesus to fulfill His plan to rescue us.

SESSION AIMS

In this session, you will guide group members to (1) read the story of the Israelites' bondage in Egypt, (2) see God's compassion as the key to their rescue, and (3) relate that deliverance to how Jesus Christ rescued us.

THE BIGGEST VERSE

"For God so loved the world that he gave his one and only son, that whoever believes in him shall not perish but have eternal life" (John 3:16).

OTHER IMPORTANT VERSES

Exodus 1–2:10; Job 42:2; Jeremiah 29:11; Matthew 6:26; Romans 8:28; 2 Corinthians 1:3; Philippians 2:12-13; 1 John 4:9-10

In the 1800s, people went west to find freedom. The vast western horizon promised such measureless opportunities that many people felt compelled to leave behind whatever was comfortable and familiar to pursue the dangerous (or at least risky) and the unknown. And many of those people did experience what they had dreamed of achieving. Through their own hard work, courage and determination to succeed, they saw the fulfillment of their plans—but not without significant trials and hardships!

Similarly, the Israelites initially realized their dreams of a land of plenty when Jacob moved his family to Egypt where they were welcomed with open arms and given good land on which to live. They prospered and increased in number and had the freedom to achieve everything they probably had imagined for themselves (see Genesis 45–50). But then came a new pharaoh, and the Egyptians started to worry that the Israelites might rise up against them. The Israelites lost their freedom and were forced into slavery, experiencing significant trials and hardships. But God had a plan for their rescue!

Likewise, we can envision the promise of freedom from sin that God offers us in His Son, Jesus, but our "moving west" toward that promise isn't easy. We often find ourselves in dry deserts, in dangerous territory, in hot spots of trouble—maybe even in what feels like a jail, staring through imaginary bars that seem to hold us back from obtaining our dreams. We often feel as if we are held captive to our sinful natures. In our own strength, we cannot deal with every trial and hardship we experience, and we cannot right the wrongs we do. But God had a plan for our rescue!

Like the oppressed Israelites of the Old Testament, we are trapped in a hot desert, held in an enemy's grasp, and we need someone to rescue us. When the Israelites "groaned . . . and cried out, . . . God heard . . . remembered . . . looked on . . . and was concerned about them" (Exodus 2:23-24). By their actions, the Israelites acknowledged their need for God's help. And because of God's great compassion, He began to work out His plan of deliverance for the Israelites. Likewise, we do not have what we need to experience freedom from sin, but because God loves us, ages ago He began to work out His plan to rescue us from that sin.

STARTER

Depend *on* Him. You'll need two boxes that lock with small keys (such as cashboxes), and candy (or some other snack food). Ahead of time, fill each box with candy and lock it. Then, freeze each key in a separate, small block of ice. (Also ahead of time, check to make sure that no one is allergic to the food you provide.) (Note: One way to get the key in the middle of a block of ice is to tie one end of clear fishing line to the key and tie the other end of the line to a pencil. Lay the pencil across the top of the water container so that the key is suspended midway in the water. Then pop the container in a freezer for a few hours.)

Welcome the group members and divide the group into two teams. Give each team a box and a block of ice with a key inside it. Explain that the task of each group is to open the box, which means they will have to get the key out of the ice by melting it. The first team to successfully open the box wins. Encourage group members to be creative about getting the key, but do not allow them to use any tools to break up the ice. The idea is for the group members to figure out what they need but to not be able to get to it. Once the ice melts and a team opens their box, declare them winners and invite both teams to enjoy the snack.

Explain that often we do not have what we need to get what we want. We might be able to see what we need, but getting it is a different story—in fact, it is the story of the human race. We have been given our lives to enjoy, but we often can't seem to get to a point where we can really be happy and not worried about anything. Difficulties, hardships, challenges of all sorts can hold us back from the experiences we know God wants us to have. We need someone to step in and do for us what we cannot do for ourselves: We need someone to get the key for us! In today's lesson, we are going to focus on how God had a plan to show His great love for us by providing the key for our rescue.

MESSAGE

Learn *from* **Him.** You will need Bibles, one copy of "Glimpse and Gaze" for each group member (found on page 13), one copy of "The Back Stories of the Israelites and Moses" for you (found on page 14), and pens or pencils.

Because this session will involve looking at the relationship between the Old and New Testaments, make sure group members understand that the Old Testament is not only a narrative of God's interactions with the Israelites but also a picture of God's eternal plan to save humankind. In the Old Testament, we catch *glimpses* of God's redemptive plan as He literally rescued His people from physical enemies (the Egyptians, the Philistines and the Babylonians); in the New Testament, we *gaze* at the fulfillment of God's plan of deliverance: the life, death and resurrection of Jesus Christ, the One who rescued us from our spiritual enemies (sin, death and Satan).

Encourage the group to think in terms of Old West storylines where a town is under the thumb of a land-hungry ranch owner who wants to control the territory. The townspeople are in need of rescuing by someone who will stand up to the ranch owner. Suddenly, on the horizon appears a stranger who rides into town just when things are getting really dicey for the townspeople.

Then explain that today's session focuses on when the Israelites were living in Egypt and were under the thumb of the pharaoh. Hand out Bibles, copies of "Glimpse and Gaze," and pens or pencils. Have pairs work together to read the passages and complete the handout. Be sure you and your helpers move around the group members, interacting with them, helping as needed and sharing your own excitement for the truth of God's Word. Once everyone is finished, gather the group members together and review their responses on the handout. Focus on the Old Testament passage first, and then relate the story of the Israelites to what we learn about faith in Jesus in the New Testament verses. Refer to "The Back Stories of the Israelites and Moses" sheet for background information as needed.

DIG

Live *for* Him. For this activity, you'll need your Bible with the following verses bookmarked: John 3:16; John 15:13; Romans 5:8; 1 John 4:15-16.

OLD WEST CHARACTERS

DANIEL BOONE (1734–1820)

Daniel Boone was a pioneer, explorer and frontiersman whose numerous exploits made him one of the first folk heroes in the United States. He is most renown for his exploration and settlement of what is now the state of Kentucky. In 1778, Boone was captured by Shawnee warriors, who, after allowing him to spend some time among them, adopted him into their tribe. He served as a militia officer during the Revolutionary War and served three terms in the Virginia General Assembly. Boone became a "legend in his own lifetime" after a book recounting his adventures was first published in 1784.

Photo: Painting by John James Audubon (1785–1851). Public domain.

The apostle Paul explained that everything from Genesis to Malachi was written "to teach us so that through endurance and the encouragement of the Scriptures we might have hope" (Romans 15:4). Look up the Old Testament passages listed below and summarize what happened. Then look up the New Testament verses and tell how those Old Testament ideas find expression in our relationship to Jesus. The first one is done as an example for you, but feel free to add to it. You're smart. You can do it.

Old Testament Glimpse	New Testament Gaze
Exodus 1:1-5: *The beginning of Exodus lists the names of the sons of Israel.*	**John 10:3,14:** *Jesus is our Shepherd, and He knows each of us by name.*
Exodus 1:6-14:	**Acts 5:12-20:**
Exodus 1:15-22:	**Galatians 5:1; John 3:16:**
Exodus 2:1-10:	**Ephesians 1:11:**

The Back Stories of the Israelites and Moses

The Israelites (Exodus 1)

The Israelites were descendants of Abraham, a man God called to be the father of a new nation, a nation that would be great in number and a blessing for all peoples (see Genesis 12:1-3). Abraham had a son named Isaac, Isaac had a son named Jacob, and Jacob had 12 sons who were the ancestors of the 12 tribes of Israel. All 12 sons and their families ended up living in Egypt under the protection of Joseph, one of the sons who worked for Pharaoh. Things were fine for a while. Over time, though, things changed. In addition to enforcing cruel oppression of the Israelites, a new pharaoh initiated an infanticide to keep the Israelite population from growing. Life was hard for the Israelites, and they did not have what they needed to help themselves.

Old Testament Glimpse	New Testament Gaze
Exodus 1:1-5: *The beginning of Exodus lists the names of the sons of Israel.*	**John 10:3,14:** *Jesus knows us by name and like a shepherd laid down His life for us.*
Exodus 1:6-14: *The Israelites were doing well, growing and prospering. Then fear of them drove the Egyptian king to treat them cruelly.*	**Acts 5:12-20:** *Even when doing good things, believers in Jesus may face jealousy and persecution from others.*
Exodus 1:15-22: *The Egyptian king ordered the Israelite midwives to kill all baby boys they delivered, but they did not do it. God rewarded them by giving them families of their own.*	**Galatians 5:1; John 3:16:** *We can show courage by standing firm in our faith in Jesus and continuing to do what is right. By faith we will have eternal life.*

Moses (Exodus 2:1-10)

Nothing ever takes God by surprise. He was at work, raising up someone to help His people: Moses. Think about all the ways in which God directed Moses' life: As a newborn, Moses wasn't discovered, even though babies tend to make a lot of noise; he wasn't harmed by crocodiles (or any other animal), even though he was in a basket on the banks of the Nile; he was adopted by a princess and raised to have an insider's understanding of the royal court, but his birth mom still got to be his nanny, so he had an insider's understanding of what it meant to be part of God's Chosen People. Unfortunately, even though Moses had been set apart from birth as a special deliverer for God's oppressed people, he did not have what he needed in and of himself to bring that deliverance about. He needed God.

Old Testament Glimpse	New Testament Gaze
Exodus 2:1-10: *Moses was one of the babies who should have been killed, but he wasn't. Through God's sovereign plan, Moses was rescued from the Nile and raised in the royal household as the son of Pharaoh's daughter.*	**Ephesians 1:11:** *Christ guides the course of our lives to accomplish His will and bring Him glory. His plan cannot be stymied by anything or anyone.*

Explain to the group that they've now seen how some of the stories in the Old Testament can be related to what the New Testament talks about. Just as the Israelites were bound in slavery, so too we are all bound in sin. And like the Israelites, we need someone to rescue us because we cannot do it for ourselves. Fortunately, God has a plan for our redemption.

Have five different volunteers read aloud the bookmarked verses in your Bible, repeating John 3:16 at the end. Ask another volunteer to tell in one word the reason God did what He did for us ("love"). God rescued us because He loves us. His compassion is the sole motivator for His plan of deliverance, or rescue, in our lives.

Invite a few group members to share ways in which they have felt God's compassion at work in their lives. (There will probably be group members who are struggling to sense God's love in their lives, so assure the group that God is faithful and will help them learn to trust that He is at work for them and in them.)

APPLY

Move *to* Him. For this activity, you'll need your Bible, one key and one 12-inch length of white ribbon for each group member, and ball-point pens.

Have a volunteer read aloud John 3:16. Explain that our most desperate need is for forgiveness—we need it but cannot get it ourselves. Sin separates us from God and prevents the relationships that God intended for us to experience, not only with Himself but also with each other. Jesus came to bear the punishment for our sins so that we could be forgiven and reconciled to the Father. God didn't *have* to save us. He *wanted* to because He loves us. Give each group member a key, a ribbon and a marker. Have them thread their ribbons through their keys and then write, "God's love is the key to my salvation," on the ribbon. Encourage the group to use their keys as reminders of God's great love for them.

End the session by praying for the group, asking God to help the group better understand His plan for them.

REFLECT

Be *with* Him. The following short devotions are for group members to reflect on and answer during the week. You can make copies of these pages and distribute them to your group members, or you can download and print the pages from **www.gospellight.com/uncommon/jh_Jesus_is_with_me.zip**.

1—GOD ANSWERS PRAYERS

Read Psalm 34. Yep . . . the whole thing. What did the psalmist do, and what did God do in return (see verse 4)?

_____

_____

_____

_____

Now read aloud Psalm 34:5-6 (yes, aloud!). How often are those who look to God for help ashamed?

_____

_____

_____

_____

How is what God does for us similar to what the mysterious stranger does for oppressed townspeople in a typical Western?

_____

_____

_____

_____

Spend a few minutes in prayer, asking God to deliver you from whatever fear you are facing. Then thank Him that since you called out to Him, He is already at work, rescuing you and working out His will to deliver you from that fear.

2—GOD BLESSES US

Read Psalm 34. Yep . . . the whole thing . . . again. In verse 8, we're invited to experience how good and loving God is. Once we realize how good God really is, how much He really loves us, it is easy to run to Him for refuge. A refuge is a place of safety and shelter. It doesn't mean that the trouble is gone, but it does mean that we have a sanctuary to hide in.

Write out five adjectives that describe God's love.

_____

_____

_____

How have you sensed God's goodness in the past year?

_____

_____

_____

_____

What will God do for those who seek His help?

_____

_____

_____

Spend a minute thanking God for His love and for the fact that He is a place of safety during times of trouble.

3—GOD DESIRES OBEDIENCE

Read Psalm 34. Yep . . . the whole thing . . . again. (Bet it's getting really familiar to you!) Verses 9,11-14 talk about fearing the Lord. What is the connection between loving God and fearing Him?

_____

_____

_____

In many Westerns, the downtrodden townspeople both fear and love the mysterious stranger who shows up to help them. How is their feeling different from the fear and love we have for God?

_____

_____

_____

To fear God is to have such awe and respect for Him that we want to do exactly what He says. When we fear Him, we obey Him; and when we obey Him, we find true refuge. Who do you fear more: people or God? Why?

_____

_____

_____

_____

Spend a few minutes in prayer, asking God to help you learn to fear Him and to find refuge in Him alone.

4—GOD RESCUES US

Read Psalm 34. Yep . . . the whole thing . . . for the last time. (Bet you can recite part of it from memory now!) According to verses 17-22, what does God do for those who obey Him and take refuge in Him?

_____

_____

_____

_____

When might you need to take refuge in God?

_____

_____

_____

_____

What are a few specific ways that you can take refuge in God?

_____

_____

_____

Spend a few minutes crying out to God for all the ways in which you need His help—for yourself, your friends, your family, your community. Then lift your hands and thank Him for His promise to hear you and to help you. Thank God too for sending Jesus to fulfill God's plan to redeem you.

ULTIMATE POWER

THE BIG IDEA

God is the ultimate source of power, and He wants to use His power to help us.

SESSION AIMS

In this session, group members will learn that (1) natural and supernatural signs reveal God's power, (2) God used His power to help His people in the past and can help us now, and (3) by God's power we will be able to spend eternity with Jesus.

THE BIGGEST VERSE

"I have told you these things, so that in me you may have peace. In this world you will have trouble. But take heart! I have overcome the world" (John 16:33).

OTHER IMPORTANT VERSES

Exodus 3–4; 17:15; Job 26:14; Psalm 24:10; Jeremiah 10:12; Matthew 19:26

There is power in a name. Jesse James, Wyatt Earp, Wild Bill Hickok, Kit Carson, Calamity Jane . . . when you hear such names from the Old West, you immediately think of entire *lives.* Sometimes these are good lives, while at other times . . . well, they are less-than-virtuous lives. But the power of a name to represent not just a person but a life and legacy is huge. God revealed His name—"the name by which [He is] to be remembered from generation to generation"—to Moses at the burning bush (Exodus 3:15). Much like each name from the Old West, God's name also signals a life. But this is an eternal, unchanging, self-sufficient life: the great I AM.

STARTER

Depend *on* Him. For this activity, ahead of time put together a PowerPoint presentation (or gather a small collection of pictures) of unusual places. (You can do this fairly easily by typing "strange places" in the search engine you use.) Your choices should inspire awe at the wild imagination of God. Be sure to note where the places are so that you can identify the places.

Welcome the group, and ask them to describe the strangest places they've ever been. Point out that what makes something strange, or unusual, is that it is not what we usually see or not what we expect. Show your PowerPoint presentation (or pictures) and invite volunteers to comment on the unexpected nature of the locations.

Explain to the group that encountering something unexpected stirs in us the idea of possibility—*After all*, we think, *if* that *exists, then why not* this*?* As human beings we are wired to believe in the impossible. In today's session, we'll discuss how Moses had a very unusual encounter that enabled him to see the divine power of God in a way that changed the course of his whole life.

MESSAGE

Learn *from* Him. For this activity, you will need Bibles; a tree branch (or a small tree, either real or fake); a bucket filled with sand; orange, red and yellow tissue paper; and tape. Ahead of time, place the tree branch in the bucket so that it stands upright. In addition, crumple the pieces of tissue paper and tape them to the tree branch to simulate flames.

Hand out Bibles so that group members can follow along as you read aloud passages from Exodus 3–4. After you read each passage, discuss its significance. Start by standing by the burning bush you created.

Read Exodus 3:1-6. Draw attention to the following sequence: (1) God initiating His encounter with Moses (verse 2); (2) Moses responding to it (verse 3); (3) God personally revealing Himself to Moses (verses 4-6a); and (4) Moses' overwhelming sense of awe at God's powerful presence (verse 6b). This is important for the group to note, because it's how God draws us to Himself as well: He initiates everything by opening our eyes to see something unusual, some aspect of His power at work in the world; we respond to that general revelation and move toward Him; He then personally reveals Himself to us; and we end with awestruck worship at how great and mighty He is.

Take a minute and allow the group to silently consider where they might be in that sequence. Have they seen a general but powerful glimpse of God and are just now moving toward it to find out more about God? Or are they awestruck with wonder at how powerful He is? (Do not necessarily ask group members to reveal out loud where they are; this is a moment for personal reflection.)

Moses' encounter with the burning bush was not a magic trick meant to impress; it wasn't God showing off. This miraculous sign allowed Moses to see more clearly the nature of the God who had watched over him from birth and who had called him to help the Israelites. Invite volunteers to tell what the fire reveals about God's power (such as: God's power is not limited by what we consider natural laws of physics; His power can be demonstrated without caus-ing destruction). Note that in verse 6, the fire is connected to holiness. This kind of revelation caused Moses to feel his own inadequacy, which was good, because like Moses, our acknowledgment of our own needs is the beginning of true repentance.

Now read Exodus 3:7-10. Invite the group to keep track of every time the pronoun "I" is used in reference to God and to note the action each time the pronoun for God is used ("I have . . . seen" [verse 7], "I have heard" [verse 7], "I am concerned" [verse 7], "I have come down" [verse 8], "I have seen" [verse 9] and "I am sending" [verse 10]).

Ask volunteers to tell what these actions reveal about the power of God (such as: God watches over His creation; God listens to His people; God re-sponds to those who are hurting; God can move around at will). In other words, God is both great and loving. We sometimes think of those with great power as being selfish and cold; our God is not! He is concerned enough to come down and help us.

Suggest to the group that they think of the Old West and how problems are solved in most of the Westerns they have seen or read. Usually a hero shows up to save the oppressed townspeople, or through his (or her) own determination and efforts, a rancher is able to make the land productive. Or the wagon train makes it to its destination because the pioneers kept moving forward in spite of the hardships they had to endure along the way. Or the cattle herd makes it to market, all due to the efforts of a few determined cowboys who refused to give in when the going got tough. Point out that in all of these scenarios, it is through human effort—human power—that success is found, the goal realized (you might also mention that these scenarios are all fiction). In the case of the Israelites, however, they needed God's help—divine power— in order to overcome their oppression; they could not overcome their situation by their own efforts (and these were *real* people).

Continue by reading Exodus 3:11-15. Point out that God's name is significant, because it reveals His nature in a unique and clarifying way. His name is not a noun, which is what a name usually is. Instead, His name is a verb—an action—and it evokes possibility: He *is*. The Hebrew phrase can be translated as "I am who I am" or "I will be what I will be." God is not limited or bound in any way. He is the eternal, self-existent Lord. Moses needed to know that a being more powerful than nature, than expectation, than oppression was the One who was calling him. The breadth of God's glory and power is seen in how He describes Himself. His name declares the power of His Being.

Have the group think of nicknames of people from the Old West and invite them to tell what the names "say" about the people. (If group members have trouble thinking of names, suggest a few, such as Billy the Kid, Calamity Jane,

---

OLD WEST CHARACTERS

WYATT EARP (1848–1929)

Wyatt Earp was an assistant city marshal in Dodge City, Kansas, before moving to Tombstone, Arizona, with his brothers, James and Virgil. Once there, the Earps clashed with a group of outlaws, culiminating in the famous "Gunfight at the O.K. Corral" on October 26, 1881. The 30-second gunfight—generally regarded as the most famous in the American Old West—was largely unknown to the public until author Stuart Lake published a largely fictionalized biography of Earp two years after his death. Today, Earp has the reputation of being "the toughest and deadliest gunman of his day."

Photo: Heritage Auction Gallery, date unknown. Public domain.

or Wild Bill Hickok). Also invite the group to tell what images come to mind when they hear names like Jesse James, Wyatt Earp or Kit Carson. Then ask volunteers to tell what comes to mind when they hear God's name, I AM. Sress that His name indicates He is a God of power and action.

Read Exodus 3:16-22. Go over what would happen as Moses stepped out and obeyed God (the elders would listen [verse 18], the king would not let the Israelites go [verse 19], God would perform miracles [verse 20], the king would let the Israelites go [verse 20], and the Egyptians would give the Israelites silver, gold and clothing [verse 22]). Emphasize how detailed God's plan was. He was not making it up on the fly, not merely having a knee-jerk response to a situation; He initiated it and completely directed it. God told Moses exactly what to do and how things would turn out.

Read Exodus 4:1-9. Note the three signs that God gave to Moses, and invite volunteers to suggest the significance of each sign: (1) The snake (verses 2-4) was a symbol to the Egyptians of royalty and divine power; thus, to see Moses' staff turn into a snake was to see that the power of God was more dominant than the power of the Egyptian kings. (2) Leprosy (verses 6-7) signaled uncleanness and, as such, meant social exclusion. This sign showed God's power over all that kept man isolated and untouchable; God's power restores relationship. (3) The Nile River (verse 9) was considered divine, so its turning into blood meant that there was a power *more* divine. To the people of that time and place, these three signs communicated the mighty power of I AM in His authority over people, disease and nature.

Emphasize to the group that each of these miracles—and every other miracle performed by God—are not magic tricks. Miracles are an outworking of the will of God for His glory alone. God can and does speak in miraculous ways. If possible, tell a story about a recent time when you either witnessed one of God's miracles or heard of one from a reliable source, focusing on the way the miracle revealed the nature and power of God.

Read Exodus 4:10-17. Note the excuses Moses gave for not doing what God wanted (not a good speaker [verse 10] and felt totally inadequate [verse 13]). Point out that Moses had already suggested that he wasn't worthy to do what God wanted (see Exodus 3:11), had claimed that he didn't even know the name of the One who was telling him to go to Egypt (see Exodus 3:13), and wasn't sure anyone would believe him (see Exodus 4:1). While God was not happy about Moses' reluctance, He didn't take back the calling. Instead, God came alongside Moses and provided support so that he could move forward. God is never offended by our weaknesses. In fact, our weaknesses provide better opportunities for God to show His power. God knew Moses would need help and had already sent Aaron to him (see verse 14).

Conclude by reading Exodus 4:18-30, and summarize how Moses began his leadership role. Finally, tell the group to think about the fact that sometimes even when we do understand how powerful God is, we may still be afraid to trust Him—just like Moses had been afraid. Invite volunteers to tell why it can still be difficult to place our faith in God's plan for us, even when we know that He has the power to fulfill it.

DIG

Live *for* **Him.** For this activity, you'll need Bibles, one copy of "God's Got a Name for That" (found on the next page) for each group member, and some pens or pencils. Hand out Bibles, pens or pencils, and copies of "God's Got a Name for That." Have pairs complete the handout. When they've finished, gather the group members back together and review their responses (use the sample answers below as a guide). Then invite a few volunteers to tell which name means the most to them right now, and why.

Scripture	Name Used to Describe God	What God Does that Is Described by His Name
Genesis 16:13	The God who sees me	He is always with me and sees everything I do.
Genesis 22:14	The Lord will provide	He meets every need I have.
Judges 6:24	The Lord is peace	He provides comfort and confidence.
1 Samuel 1:3	The Lord Almighty	He is the most powerful being and has power over everything in the universe.
Jeremiah 23:6	The Lord Our Righteousness	He blesses us and makes us holy.
1 Peter 2:25	The Shepherd and Overseer of [our] souls	He guides and protects me. He cares about me spiritually and physically.

GoD's GoT A NAME FoR THAT

God told Moses that His name is "I AM WHO I AM" (Exodus 3:14). More than just a label, God's name speaks to us of His nature and His power and of our relationship to Him: He is the One who exists eternally and is unchanging. What are some of the things about God that are unchanging?

_____

_____

_____

_____

Look up the following passages and identify the name given to or used to describe God. Then tell what God does that reflects for us the meaning of that name

Scripture	Name Used to Describe God	What God Does that Is Described by His Name
Genesis 16:13	The God who sees me.	He is always with me and knows everything that I do.
Genesis 22:14		
Judges 6:24		
1 Samuel 1:3		
Jeremiah 23:6		
1 Peter 2:25		

APPLY

Move *to* **Him**. For this activity, you'll need unlined index cards, markers in various colors, glue, and two small flat magnets for each group member.

God was concerned enough to "come down" and help the Israelites (Exodus 3:8). This foreshadowed what Jesus would do for us. Read aloud John 1:14. Jesus "came from the Father [came down from heaven], full of grace and truth," to rescue us from our sins so that we can be restored to the Father. That in and of itself is marvelous, but as Christians, we have reason to be even more amazed: God has the power to raise us up so that we spend eternity with Him! We have a sinful nature, and we simply cannot get rid of our sins through our own efforts. We need God's power to help us.

Read aloud John 16:33. No matter what hardships we have to endure, Jesus is always with us. When we believe in Him, we can have peace during trying times, because Jesus already claimed victory for us. Jesus died for our sins, but "by his power God raised the Lord from the dead, and he will raise us also" (1 Corinthians 6:14). God's power is so great that He overcame death itself. And He will do the same for all those who believe in Jesus and obey Him.

Show the group how two of the magnets you brought attract each other and stick together. Point out that the power the magnets have is obviously not as strong as the power God has, but the magnets can be used to remind us of God's power.

Hand out to each group member an index card and two magnets, and arrange the other materials so that group members can share them. Instruct the group to take the index card and fold it in half. On one of the halves facing out from the fold, each group member should draw a powerful object (either manmade or natural); on the other side facing out, group members should write, "Take heart! I have overcome the world (John 16:33)." Then the group members should glue to the inside of the index card the two magnets, one on each half inside the fold, so that the magnets stick together. Then show the group members how to open the card, slide it over a page in the Bible (or any book) and let the magnets stick together, thus marking the page.

End the session by praying for the group, asking God to continue to use His power to help them.

REFLECT

Be *with* **Him**. The following short devotions are for group members to reflect on and answer during the week. You can make copies of these pages and distribute them to your group members, or you can download and print the pages from **www.gospellight.com/uncommon/jh_Jesus_is_with_me.zip.**

1—POWER IN CREATION

Read Romans 1:20. Why should no one doubt the existence of God?

_____

_____

_____

_____

_____

_____

What did God do to create the universe? (Note: If you need a reminder, turn to Genesis 1.)

_____

_____

_____

_____

_____

When we recognize the mighty power He displayed by His acts of creation, how should we regard God (if you need help with the answer, see Psalm 33:1-2,8)?

_____

_____

_____

_____

_____

Take a minute to try to imagine being present when God first created everything and the amount of power He displayed. Then thank God for the things He created that you like best.

2—POWER IN A NAME

Read Exodus 3:14. What does God's name reveal about God's power?

_____

_____

_____

_____

Sometimes in the Old West, a person's name by itself had the power to scare people because of what people imagined when they heard it—what they imagined might happen, what they thought the person had done, and so on. Why should God's great power be a comfort to us?

_____

_____

_____

_____

Read Psalms 5:11 and 8:1. What do these verses say about God's name and how we should react to it?

_____

_____

_____

_____

Take a minute to realize how important it is to never misuse God's name, and then thank God that He revealed His name to Moses (and to us!).

3—POWER OVER DEATH

Let's take John 16:33 piece by piece, shall we? What does "in me you may have peace" mean?

_____

_____

_____

What does "in this world you will have trouble" mean?

_____

_____

_____

_____

_____

What does "take heart" mean, and why specifically can we do that?

_____

_____

_____

_____

_____

Take a minute to thank Jesus for what He did for us. Then pray that God would make you His today, fully and completely.

4—POWER IN VICTORY

Read Ephesians 1:19-22. Why can we be sure that God has won the final victory (see verses 20-22)?

_____

_____

_____

_____

_____

To whom is God's power available (see verse 19)?

_____

_____

_____

_____

_____

How does that truth influence your view of your life?

_____

_____

_____

_____

_____

God wants you to know Him and call on Him. God and His power are always available to you. Take a minute to ask Him to use His power to help today with whatever is troubling you or someone you know.

ULTIMATE RESCUE

THE BIG IDEA

God rescued the Israelites at Passover, and Jesus is the eternal Passover Lamb who rescued us from sin and gives us eternal life.

SESSION AIMS

In this session, group members will learn that (1) God saved His people from slavery in Egypt, (2) Jesus saved us from slavery to sin, and (3) we can receive the gift of eternal life

THE BIGGEST VERSE

"I am the resurrection and the life. He who believes in me will live, even though he dies" (John 11:25).

OTHER IMPORTANT VERSES

Exodus 5–12; John 3:15; 14:6,19; Romans 5:9; 1 Corinthians 5:7; Ephesians 2:8,13; Hebrews 9:22

Many of the storylines in Westerns have to do with people in need of being res-cued. It could be a town full of people who are being forced to live under the thumb of an unscrupulous landowner who wants to control everything and everyone in the territory. Or it could be a damsel in distress, one who is being forced to abandon the family ranch because of a banker who is trying to coerce her into marrying him. Or it could be a hard-working family just trying to find a place of their own to homestead and raise sheep, but the locals don't want them or their animals "ruining" the grazing land for the local cattle herds. So they harass the new folks and try to get them to leave the area.

The oppressed townspeople, the damsel in distress and the hard-working family fret and talk about what they need with friends and family, but they can't do anything on their own. They need a hero, a lone cowboy who rides to the rescue in each situation. In the same way, the Israelites, forced into slavery by Pharaoh in Egypt, fretted and talked about their situation—but they talked to God. And God had a plan to rescue the Israelites, just like He had a plan to res-cue us from our sins and make it possible for us to have eternal life.

STARTER

Depend *on* **Him.** You'll need one light-colored cowboy hat and one dark-colored cowboy hat (one black hat and one white hat would be ideal) and plenty of room to move.

Welcome the group, and then tell the group that they're going to play a variation of Freeze Tag that focuses on the idea of immunity. Invite one volun-teer to be the Landowner and wear the dark-colored hat, and invite the rest of the group to be the Townspeople. Hand the light-colored hat to one of the townspeople. Explain that whoever is wearing the light-colored hat has immu-nity and cannot be tagged. The hat also has the power to release a team mem-ber who has been frozen. The hat can be passed around as needed—whatever will be strategic to the Townspeople's cause. At your signal, Landowner tries to tag as many Townspeople as possible. Whenever a Townsperson is tagged, he or she must freeze in place. Let the group play until you call time.

Explain that in today's session, the group will be reading about the Exodus and the Passover, when God rescued His Chosen People from slavery in Egypt. The Hebrew word for "Passover" actually means "pass over," the idea of being exempt or immune from penalty, of being spared. In the game of tag the group just played, the light-colored hat provided immunity from the penalty of being tagged, and it brought back to life a person who had been frozen.

During the Passover, God had great compassion for His Chosen People and was moved to grant them immunity from death—not because of what they could do or how they could repay Him, but simply because He is good and powerful and loving. Similarly, what Jesus chose to do for us on the cross granted us immunity from the punishment our sins would normally warrant.

MESSAGE

Learn *from* **Him.** For this activity, you'll need Bibles, a copy of "A Long, Hard Rescue" (found on the pages 35-36) for every group member, and pens or pencils

Welcome the group members, and invite volunteers to recall some of the details about Moses from the previous two sessions (saved as a baby; raised in Pharaoh's household, but own mother was nanny; met God at the burning bush and chosen by God to help the Israelites; shown signs by God; reluctant to do God's bidding; Aaron sent by God to help him). Remind the group that Moses was the first person to know God by His name, I AM.

Explain that today's session involves a look at how I AM rescued the Israelites from their slavery in Egypt. Hand out copies of "A Long, Hard Rescue" and pens or pencils. Have groups of three to four members work together to complete the handout. The questions on the handout cover a large section of the book of Exodus, so be sure to move among the groups and offer help as needed. After everyone has completed the handout, gather the group together and go over the handout to review God's rescue of the Israelites.

As you review, point out to the group that the need the Israelites had to be rescued is not unlike the plot of many stories about the Old West. Many Westerns deal with an injustice—in one form or another—that needs to be corrected. The oppressed people in these situations know they can't fix their situations by themselves, but they are at a loss about what to do or where to turn. Then, suddenly, who should appear but a lone cowboy riding into town (or onto the ranch land). That lone cowboy, it just so happens, will save the day because he is more experienced and can do what needs to be done. Fortunately, the Israelites had someone even more powerful and more experienced to come to their rescue!

As you discuss the story, guide the group to see that through these events, God revealed His authority over earthly kings, magical powers and the cruel way in which His people were being treated. He revealed His ability to distinguish between His Chosen People and the Egyptians, to decree the timing of both plagues and rescue, to provide for His people from the wealth of those oppressing them. Nothing happened by chance. Everything that happened occurred because of God's plan and through God's power to show God's glory.

DIG

Live *for* Him. For this activity you will need matzo, napkins, a bottle of grated horseradish, craft sticks or popsicle sticks, parsley and salty water. (Check ahead of time that no group member has an allergy to any food you provide.) (Other foods you might consider providing include Romaine lettuce, charoset and hard-boiled eggs.)

Pass out the matzo and napkins for the group members to snack on as you describe some of the foods eaten at a Seder (Passover meal). Invite a few volunteers to sample the horseradish by dipping a tongue depressor into the bottle in order to retrieve a small sample. Invite a few other volunteers to dip the parsley into the salty water before eating it.

As volunteers sample the foods, explain that in order to commemorate God's rescue of the Israelites from slavery in Egypt, every year people of the Jewish faith celebrate Passover, starting with a meal called the Seder. Special foods are used to symbolize parts of the Passover event, including bitter herbs (to symbolize the bitterness of the slavery the Israelites suffered at the hands of the Egyptians); a sweet fruit and nut paste (to represent the mortar used in the buildings constructed by the Israelites); a vegetable dipped in salty water (to remind people

---

OLD WEST CHARACTERS

MARY FIELDS (c. 1832–1914)

Mary Fields, also known as "Stagecoach Mary," was the first African-American woman employed as a mail carrier in the United States. Fields obtained the job in 1895 at the age of 60 because she was the fastest applicant to hitch a team of six horses. She drove her route from Cascade to St. Peter's Mission in Montana for several years and, despite heavy snowfalls that sometimes forced her to deliver mail on foot, never once missed a day. She retired at the age of 70 and ultimately became a respected public figure in the town of Cascade. She died in 1914, at just over the age of 80, from liver failure.

Photo: Unknown, circa 1895. Public domain.

A LONG, HARD RESCUE

Exodus 5 records the start of the Exodus ball rolling in Egypt as Moses and Aaron first ask Pharaoh to let the Israelites leave Egypt. But it isn't until Exodus 12 that the Israelites' being brought out of Egypt by God is recorded. A lot of stuff happened in-between. To discover what the "stuff" was, quickly read through or skim the passages below and then answer the questions.

EXODUS 5. Sometimes things go from bad to worse, even when we are doing exactly what we should. What happened as a result of the request Moses and Aaron made of Pharaoh?

_____

_____

_____

_____

EXODUS 6:1–7:6. It's good to know that when we doubt, God doesn't reject us; instead, He reaffirms His truth so that we will have the courage we need to follow Him. What are all the things God says He'll do for His people (see Exodus 6:1-8)?

_____

_____

_____

_____

EXODUS 7:6-13. This event sets the stage for the 10 plagues that follow. It wasn't just a magician's showdown; it was a revelation of the One true God. What does it suggest about God's power (see especially verse 12)?

_____

_____

_____

_____

EXODUS 7:14–11. The next several chapters of the book of Exodus describe the 10 plagues that God made happen. Skim through those chapters and complete this chart so that you know what each plague was, who suffered from the plague (Egyptians and Israelites or only Egyptians?) and what Pharaoh's response was to each one.

Passage	Plague	Who Suffered	Pharoh's Response
Exodus 7:14-25			
Exodus 8:1-15			
Exodus 8:16-19			
Exodus 8:20-32			
Exodus 9:1-7			
Exodus 9:8-12			
Exodus 9:13-35			
Exodus 10:1-20			
Exodus 10:21-29			
Exodus 11; 12:29-32			

EXODUS 7:3-5; 9:16. Why did God harden Pharaoh's heart?

_____

_____

_____

EXODUS 12. Briefly describe what the Israelites were to do so that they would be safe when God passed through Egypt and brought about the last plague.

_____

_____

_____

_____

What did God say the Israelites should do in the future, and why (see Exodus 12:42)?

_____

_____

_____

of the tears the Israelites cried because of their oppression); matzo (to signify the unleavened bread with which the Israelites fled Egypt); and a lamb bone (to symbolize the sacrificial offering of the lamb for each family).

Go on to point out that just as physical death passed over those who had the blood of the lamb on their doorposts in Egypt, spiritual death passes over those whose hearts are marked by the forgiveness of the true Passover Lamb, Jesus Christ.

Note for the group that there are several very distinct connections between the Old Testament Passover lamb and Jesus. Invite two volunteers to read each pair of verses below, one reading the Old Testament verses and the other reading the New Testament verses. After each set of verses, spend a minute helping group members make the connections between the two.

1. Exodus 12:3; John 1:29—It had to be a lamb.
2. Exodus 12:5; 1 Peter 1:18-19—The lamb had to be without defect.
3. Exodus 12:6; Matthew 27:45-50—The lamb must be offered in the early evening. (The ninth hour is 3:00 PM, which means Jesus died sometime in the late afternoon/early evening.)
4. Exodus 12:46; John 19:31-33—There would be no broken bones.
5. Exodus 12:8-11; John 6:53-56—The lamb must be eaten.
6. Exodus 12:7,13; Matthew 26:28—The lamb's blood was the sign of salvation.

Explain that the story of the Exodus is a picture of our deliverance through the death of Jesus. As the old hymn goes: "What can wash away my sin? Nothing but the blood of Jesus; What can make me whole again? Nothing but the blood of Jesus." The lamb's blood that signified that the Israelites be spared from death visiting their doors during God's pass over is reflected in the Lamb's (Jesus') blood that spares us from spiritual death. God's plan of rescue holds true for us today as much as it did for the Israelites all those hundreds of years ago.

APPLY

Move to Him. For this activity, you'll need for each group member a small wooden cross, letter beads for the word "amen" and a 30" length of cord.

Tell the group that one thing we clearly see in the Exodus of the Israelites from Egypt is that they couldn't do anything on their own to make their rescue happen. But God could, and He did—His plan, His way, His rescue, His glory.

Read aloud John 11:25. Invite a group member to tell what "believing in someone" means (to consider the person trustworthy, to firmly believe that what the person says is true. It's like a loud "Yes! That's right!"). Point out that our word "amen" is related to the Hebrew word for "believe" (*emunah*). So when we say "amen," we are asserting our belief—our trust—in what was said.

When God reveals Himself to us, we have the opportunity to believe Him, to pass from slavery to freedom, from death to life—from a life oppressed by our sinful nature to an eternity with God in heaven. Like the lamb's blood the Israelites put on their doorposts in order to be rescued, our Passover Lamb, Jesus, spilled His blood for us on the cross. Hand out crosses, letter beads and lengths of cord. Instruct group members to string the beads and the cross onto the cord to make necklaces. As the group works, remind the group that to believe in Christ, the Passover Lamb, is to say "amen" to what He did to rescue us. (As the group works, you might consider having the group sing or listen to an appropriate hymn, such as "Nothing but the Blood," "The Solid Rock" or "When I Survey the Wondrous Cross.")

End the session by praying for the group, thanking God for sending Jesus to the rescue and asking Him to strengthen everyone's belief in Christ.

REFLECT

Be *with* Him. The following short devotions are for the group members to reflect on and answer during the week. You can make copies of these pages and distribute them to your group members, or you can download and print the pages from **www.gospellight.com/uncommon/jh_Jesus_is_with_me.zip.**

1—FOREVER LOVING

Read Psalm 136. This psalm is recited at the end of the Seder at Passover. It's often referred to as the "Great Hallel," or "Great Praise." What specific events are referred to in verses 5-9?

_____

_____

_____

_____

_____

What specific events are referred to in verses 10-16?

_____

_____

_____

What are some of the differences between a lone cowboy who rescues the oppressed in a Western movie or book and God who rescued the Israelites?

_____

_____

_____

Psalm 136 is a song that celebrates God's creative, redeeming power and His enduring love. Read aloud verses 23-26 as a prayer of thanksgiving. Then go your merry way, remembering that God's love never runs out!

2—FOREVER HELPFUL

Read Psalm 113, another psalm recited during the Seder. Notice that verses 1-4 tell how awesome, great and powerful God is. Then verses 5-9 show our powerful God bending down to help people who are lowly, humble and not particularly well thought of by others. What does God do to help these people?

_____

_____

_____

How do these "small deliverances" teach us to trust God for "big deliverance"?

_____

_____

_____

What's one small way God has helped you this week?

_____

_____

_____

3—FOREVER WORTHY

Read Psalm 116, another psalm recited during the Seder. What reasons does the author of the psalm give for loving God (see verses 1-6)?

_____

_____

_____

_____

What reason does the author give for feeling at peace, even during times of trouble (see verses 7-11)?

_____

_____

_____

What should be our response to God for all of the things that He has done for us (see verses 12-19)?

_____

_____

_____

Take a minute to think of all that God has done for you and praise Him!

4—FOREVER FAMILY

Read Ephesians 1:5-8. What relationship do we have to God?

_____

_____

_____

_____

What was offered as a ransom to buy us back, or redeem us, from slavery to sin?

_____

_____

_____

Spend a minute thanking God for what our Redeemer, Jesus, did for us!

ULTIMATE TRUST

THE BIG IDEA

We can rely on God to take care of us.

SESSION AIMS

In this session, group members will (1) consider the way God provided for the Israelites while they wandered in the desert, (2) realize that we can depend on God to take care of our every need, and (3) trust Jesus to provide whatever we need.

THE BIGGEST VERSE

"I am the bread of life, he who comes to me will never go hungry, and he who believes in me will never be thirsty" (John 6:35).

OTHER IMPORTANT VERSES

Exodus 16–17:7; John 4:13-14; 6:48-51; Ephesians 3:12; Philippians 4:19; Hebrews 11:22

The average person in the United States usually has no trouble whatsoever obtaining a variety of foods to eat, whether it is from school cafeterias or coffee shops, from grocery stores or big-box stores, from fast-food chains or fancy sit-down restaurants—and, of course, from home!

But cowboys of the Wild West simply couldn't get whatever they wanted whenever they wanted it. Originally, a cowboy on a cattle drive made his own meals from what he could carry in his saddlebags. Once the chuck wagon came into being, sustenance was limited to what the chuck wagon had available to cook for the meals—breakfast and dinner—served to the drovers. Meals were usually made up of stews, steaks, beans and/or bacon, potatoes, onions, biscuits and coffee.[1] The cook tried to provide some variety, sometimes by adding food that was gathered along the way, but the meals were pretty much the same. But the cowboys ate it all without complaining!

When God led the Israelites to freedom, they began a trek across a desert that would last 40 years. During that time, God provided for them in miraculous ways time and time again—from bread, meat and water to protection and guidance. It was His faithfulness that supplied them with all that they required to get where He planned they should go. We can learn from their story that we can trust our God to not only save us but also to provide for us.

STARTER

Depend *on* Him. For this activity, you'll need some rocks (or a metal fire pit); orange, red and yellow tissue paper crumpled to look like a fire; and marshmallows. (Ahead of time, check to make sure that no one is allergic to the food you provide.) Arrange the crumpled tissue paper inside the rocks so that you make a pretend campfire.

Welcome the group, and then invite them to sit around the "campfire," just as the cowboys did when they ate while on a cattle drive. Have group members form a large circle with everyone sitting facing the campfire. Create a steady rhythm by having group members slap their thighs twice, clap their hands twice and snap their fingers twice. Once the rhythm (slap-slap-clap-clap-snap-snap) is established, have one group member begin the game by naming aloud, while snapping, an item essential to camping.

Moving to the left, the next group member, on the next set of snaps, tells another item needed for camping. Play continues around the circle, with each group member telling an item without repeating anything said before. Any group member who repeats something or doesn't say anything on the snaps is out. After a winner is determined, pass out marshmallows for everyone to eat as a snack.

MESSAGE

Learn *from* Him. For this activity, you'll need your Bible.

Invite a couple of group members to share times when they have gone camping and forgotten something. (Also be ready with a story or two of your own!) Have them tell what they did when they had no resources available and couldn't replace the missing item (most likely, they did without!).

Note to the group that in the Old West, any supplies that were forgotten when the chuck wagon was loaded for the trail had to be done without. And when supplies ran out, the same thing applied: The cowboys did without. Then point out that when God rescued the Israelites from slavery in Egypt and the Israelites began a long journey through the desert, it wasn't long before their provisions ran out. During this difficult time, they had to learn to trust that the God who had redeemed them would also provide for them. God doesn't save us and then send us off on our own to figure things out for ourselves. No! He continues to guide us—and to grow us—so that we can come to know Him. And this is exactly what He did for the Israelites!

Summarize for the group how Moses led the Israelites out of Egypt, through the Red Sea and to the desert on their way to the Promised Land. (Interestingly, they took the bones of Joseph with them—so Joseph got out of Egypt, too! Hebrews 11:22 says it was because of Joseph's faith in God's deliverance that he gave orders about taking his bones when they left: Joseph was confident that God would fulfill His promise to Abraham and give the Israelites the Promised Land!) Point out that God had demonstrated divine provision for His people in many ways: Not only did He get them out of Egypt, but He also showed them a safe route; He led them with a pillar of cloud during the day and a pillar of fire during the night, so they knew where they were supposed to go; and He destroyed the Egyptians who had come out to stop their escape. God was clearly establishing Himself as a faithful provider so they could learn to trust Him.

After about six weeks of walking through the desert toward the Promised Land, the Israelites began to get a bit tired and provisions started to run low. So what did they do? Read aloud Exodus 16:2-3. Comment to the group that rather than think about the amazing ways that God had provided for them and trust that He would continue to do so, the people started to complain. And not just complain. Their whining totally skewed reality.

Invite a volunteer to tell whether they think the Israelites in Egypt had really "sat around pots of meat" and ate all the food they wanted. Then invite a few group members to share times when their complaining didn't really reflect the truth about a situation. Guide them to see that when people are feeling distressed, they sometimes have a hard time seeing what is real. Unbelief then distorts their reality and keeps them from trusting what they know to be true.

Read aloud Exodus 16:4-5. God graciously responded to their complaining, not with judgment, but with provision. He promised to send food for them, but He was going to use the opportunity to continue to teach them to trust Him as their provider.

Read aloud Exodus 16:11-18. Note for the group that in order to teach the Israelites they had to live by faith every day, God set up the provision so they could only collect enough manna to last one day; otherwise, it would spoil. Those who got greedy and gathered more than as instructed found a nice fat bag of maggots munching the spoiled manna in the morning (see verse 20). In the Old West, food didn't keep very well either (don't forget that they didn't have coolers back then!), and only food that would keep for a long time was taken in the chuck wagon. Any meat that was taken on the trail had to be salted so that it would not become rancid. Fortunately for the cowboys, their food supply could be supplemented by what they could forage, fish for or hunt down—if they had the time. The Israelites, though, were in a desert, and their resources were very limited.

OLD WEST CHARACTERS

DAVY CROCKETT (1786–1836)

David Crockett, the "King of the Wild Frontier," was a frontiersman, soldier and politician. At the age of 13 Crockett ran away from home and spent the next three years roaming from town to town in Tennessee, where he learned many of his skills as a hunter and trapper. He joined the Tennessee Militia in 1813 and was elected to Congress in 1826. While in office he was a vocal critic of the policies of Andrew Jackson (most notably the Indian Removal Act), which led to his defeat in 1834. He moved to Texas (then an independent state of Mexico) and was killed at the Battle of the Alamo in March 1836.

Photo: Painting by John Gadsby Chapman (1808-1889). Public domain.

You would think that at this point, having seen God deliver them from Pharaoh, guide them across a desert, and bring meat and bread to them daily, the Israelites would have trusted God as their provider. Nope.

Read aloud Exodus 17:3-7. Here again, when the people needed water, God provided what they needed. Point out that Horeb is where Moses saw the burning bush. Moses was back at a place very special to him, the one where he had met I AM. I AM showed Himself to be the provider for His people, giving them all that they needed to follow Him.

Invite group members to tell what this story shows them about a life of faith. Remind them that Jesus, when He taught His disciples to pray, instructed them to ask for *"daily* bread" (Matthew 6:11, emphasis added). One of the main points of following Jesus on this earth is growing in a *daily* walk of trust. We build up our faith as we watch, day in and day out, God provide for us.

Invite the group to suggest reasons people refuse to trust God when He has shown Himself to be a faithful provider. Be careful not to let any group members feel guilty about any lack of trust they may have shown; rather, focus the discussion on people in general. Emphasize the fact that God's provision sometimes requires our obedience, like gathering the manna did for the Israelites, but we can trust that He will give us all that we need.

DIG

Live *for* Him. For this activity, you will need Bibles, a copy of "Never Really Stuck" (found on the next two pages) for each group member, and also pens or pencils.

Comment that in today's Bible story, there was a fairly predictable pattern of behavior, one even people today experience: difficulty led to complaining, which led to prayer, which led to provision, which led to trust. Hand out Bibles, copies of "Never Really Stuck," and pens or pencils. Have group members work independently to complete the handout.

After everyone is done, gather the group members back together and review their answers. Without embarrassing anyone, ask if any volunteers are willing to share which part of the cycle they are in right now. Suggest to the group that they encourage each other to keep moving forward, no matter where they are at the moment. God is teaching them about His faithfulness and as long as they don't quit, they will see Him continue to provide in miraculous ways.

Never Really Stuck

Great deeds in the past have significance for all generations. This means that when we read about people in the past, we can learn a lot from how they responded—whether in good or, well, not-so-good ways—to their situations.

The Israelites got stuck in a bad cycle: difficulty led to complaining, complaining led to prayer, prayer led to provision, provision led to trust. God was trying to teach them about His faithfulness, but there was no book He could have them buy about it! They had to learn from personal experience. Lucky for us, their experiences are described in the Bible, and we can read about their lives and learn from them so that our personal experiences aren't so rough.

Difficulty: Something that causes us pain or distress; a time of great challenge when we might question what we believe to be true. What difficulty have you faced recently or are facing right now?

_____

_____

_____

_____

Complaining: Expressing unhappiness about whatever is giving us difficulty. When we come up against difficult circumstances, we can either continue to trust or we can start to complain. What's one time you trusted? One time you complained? What was the outcome of each situation?

_____

_____

_____

_____

Prayer: Words spoken aloud or silently to God; a conversation with God. Whatever the situation, we need to go to the One who has promised not only to save but also to provide. Whether we complain or trust, we must go to God and seek His help. Write out a short prayer—it can include a complaint!—asking for wisdom to properly respond to the difficulty you are facing. God is never put off by our struggle to believe; in fact, He welcomes it as a chance to show us how good He really is.

_____

_____

_____

_____

_____

_____

Provision: Whatever we need. God is able to provide all that we need; we just need to ask Him. This doesn't mean that things always go the way we want, though. Sometimes we can't see the bigger picture and don't realize at the time how God is answering our prayers. However, we have lots of proof that God can and does provide—from the Bible and our own lives. What is it that you think you need God to provide? What can you do to help resolve the difficulty?

_____

_____

_____

_____

_____

_____

Trust: Confidence or reliance on someone or something. God urges us to lay our fears and our desires at His feet and trust Him, no matter what. Read Proverbs 3:5-6. When you trust God, what will He do? What are a few specific ways that you can show that you trust God to provide what you need?

_____

_____

_____

_____

_____

_____

APPLY

Move *to* Him. For this activity, you'll need delicious sliced bread and cups of cool refreshing water. (Ahead of time, check to make sure that no one is allergic to the food you provide.)

Hold up the bread and explain that many of the Old Testament stories not only hold a life lesson for us as followers of Jesus, but they also give us a picture of a specific aspect of the nature of Jesus. The story today about the manna from heaven is a prime example of this. Read aloud John 6:35. Invite volunteers to explain the difference between the bread from heaven that the Israelites ate and the bread from heaven that is Jesus. Give each group member a piece of bread and explain that just as our bodies need physical food to live, our spirits need divine food to live. Jesus lived and died to bring us out of darkness and death and into light and life. However, in order to grow and be spirtually healthy, we need to make Him a part of our lives each day.

Hold up a cup of water, and invite volunteers to explain the difference between the water that came from a rock when the Israelites were thirsty and the water that Jesus is able to provide. Point out that when we believe in Jesus, we receive eternal forgiveness and unending provision. Hand out cups of water for the group to enjoy.

Comment to the group that the bread and water serve as symbols to help us understand that we can trust that God will provide for us everything we truly need, even when times are difficult.

End the session by praying for the group, asking God to build up their trust that He will provide for them and take care of them every day.

REFLECT

Be *with* Him. The following short devotions are for group members to reflect on and answer during the week. You can make copies of these pages and distribute them to your group members, or you can download and print the pages from **www.gospellight.com/uncommon/jh_Jesus_is_with_me.zip.**

1—NOT-SO-LITTLE CRYBABY

If you've ever had to babysit an infant, you know this routine: The baby gets hungry, the baby screams for food, you scramble for something suitable (*not* your leftover soda), you feed the baby, the baby is quiet again.

This might seem annoying, but you do it too—even at your age! You suddenly realize you don't have something you need, you start whining or crying about it to God, God listens to you, God provides what you need, you are happy again.

In both scenarios, the point is not the crying baby but the one providing for the baby. The time when we have needs is the time when God shows us just how good He really is and how He can and will provide for us. Read James 1:2-8. What attitude should we have when we have difficulties (see verse 2)?

_____

_____

_____

_____

What does the testing of our faith produce, and why is that important (see verses 3-4)?

_____

_____

_____

_____

How does God give His wisdom? And when we ask for wisdom, what must we *not* do (see verses 5-8)?

_____

_____

_____

_____

The bottom line? Go ahead and cry! God is right there to listen and to help. He loves to provide for His children's needs.

2—BACKGROUND CHECK

One reason the Israelites started complaining about their lack of food was that they forgot all that God had done in the past to provide for them. What do you think would have happened to a cowboy who always complained about the food the cook provided on the trail?

_____

_____

_____

_____

_____

_____

Take a minute and think about how God has supplied the things you need. List at least six ways God has provided for you.

1. _____

2. _____

3. _____

4. _____

5. _____

6. _____

If this is how the Lord has been in the past, why would you think He would stop now? Why do you think some people *do* stop believing?

_____

_____

_____

_____

_____

Read Hebrews 13:8. Take a minute and thank God for the fact that He has been a good provider and will always be a good provider. Thank Him too for your being able to trust that He will never change.

3—UNLIMITED SUPPLY

Read Mark 6:30-44. The cook in charge of the chuck wagon on a cattle drive in the Old West had only limited supplies at his fingertips. In the situation described in this passage in Mark, in what ways were the disciples like the cattle-drive cook?

_____

_____

_____

_____

What would you have said if Jesus had asked you to feed that crowd? Probably something similar to His disciples: "What?! Are you kidding? I can't afford that!" How do you usually react when you have been given something that you think is impossible to do?

_____

_____

_____

_____

_____

Fortunately, it's not about what we have but about what God can do with what we have. Even when our resources seem insufficient, when God blesses them, they are more than enough. Why do you think Jesus fed the crowd instead of just sending them home?

_____

_____

_____

_____

_____

Take a minute and thank God that He is concerned about our physical needs as well as our spiritual needs. Then trust our provider God, not your provisions.

4—COMMITMENT

Remember the manna? Even though it fell from the sky supernaturally, the Israelites had to get up and gather it. There was a bit of effort—something to do—on their part in order to experience the blessing God had provided. Read Psalm 37:3-6. What are a few specific ways that you can show that you "delight" in God (verse 4)?

_____

_____

_____

_____

_____

How does a person "commit [his or her] way to the LORD," and how does this display trust in God as the best provider (verse 5)?

_____

_____

_____

_____

_____

What will God do when you trust in Him (see verse 6)?

_____

_____

_____

_____

_____

Take a minute to thank God that when we trust Him with everything we have, He will guide us in the way He knows is best.

Note

1. "The Chuck Wagon—Real Queen of the Cattle Trail," *Legends of America,* 2003-2012. http://www.legendsofamerica.com/we-chuckwagon.html (accessed December 2012).

ULTIMATE LOVE

THE BIG IDEA

God wants us to follow His commandments, which were summed up by Jesus: Love God and love each other.

SESSION AIMS

In this session, group members will (1) learn how and why God gave the Israelites the Ten Commandments, (2) see how those commandments are summed up in Jesus' teaching, and (3) commit to growing in obedience to God's Word.

THE BIGGEST VERSES

"A new commandment I give to you: Love one another. As I have loved you, so you must love one another. By this all men will know that you are my disciples, if you love one another" (John 13:34-35).

OTHER IMPORTANT VERSES

Exodus 19–20:21; 24:12; 25:10-22; Matthew 5:43-44; 22:34-40; John 6:29; Romans 13:8; 1 John 4:16

It took a great deal of trust to live as a cowboy in the Old West. Think about it: You spent from sunrise to sunset in a saddle riding a horse on a dusty trail; you were subjected to blazing heat and bitter cold, and separated from civilized life; you drove ahead of you a herd of stubborn cattle, watching constantly for attacks from nefarious robbers, rustlers, and wild animals; and you were dependent on your partners to stick around until the job was done. Traveling an average of 12 to 15 miles a day, you could be on the trail for months and months to get to your destination.

Fortunately for the cowboy, a Code of the West developed to articulate the kind of behavior these rough and rugged men could expect from one another. This came in particularly handy, because, generally speaking, there was no law out on the cattle trail. But with these unwritten rules of conduct, the cowboy could expect respect, truthfulness, kindness, diligence and fairness. Having a code enabled these men to move forward in faith, even when it was hard, and to rely upon their fellow cowboys.

God gave His rules of conduct—a God Code, if you will—to His people, revealing His nature and His will so that we would know what God expects from us and so that we would know what to expect from others. Moses brought God's words to the Israelites, who, while they struggled to believe and obey at times, did voice their faith and follow God's plan.

God gave us His commandments so that we could be connected to Him in a way that brings about not only personal blessing but also Kingdom success. And learning to obey His commandments is vital to a growing relationship with Jesus, who gave us, not a new command, but a summation of the Ten Commandments.

STARTER

Depend *on* Him. For this activity, you'll need two sheets of paper, pens or pencils, and two kinds of snacks for prizes. (Ahead of time, check to make sure that no one is allergic to the food you provide.)

Welcome the group members, have them divide into two smaller groups, and then hand each small group a sheet of paper and a pen or pencil. Explain that you are going to give both groups about 10 minutes to come up with a list of 10 Cowboy Commandments—rules that would make a cowboy's life more enjoyable. (If the groups have trouble thinking of ideas, give them a couple of examples: "Never steal a man's horse," "Always drink upstream from the herd.")

Call time and then have each group share their ideas. Decide which commandments are the most creative, and let the winning group choose first the snack they would like; then award the remaining snack to the other group. Explain that rules, while they may at times seem to be a burden, actually promote better, more successful lives. Rules can help more than they hinder! When God delivered His people from Egypt and led them into the desert, one of the things He did was to give the Israelites a set of rules to enable them to live better lives—ones that brought blessing and success.

MESSAGE

Learn *from* Him. For this activity, you will need Bibles, 10 poster boards, a marker, a CD with the sound effects of loud thunder, a CD with the sound of a loud trumpet blast that gets louder as it continues, and a CD player. Ahead of time, on one side of each poster board write one of the Ten Commandments. On the other side write the Commandment number. Tape the posters with the numbers side showing in order along the front of your meeting space. Cue the CD to play the thunder.

Invite volunteers to recap what they know about the Exodus from the previous sessions (slavery in Egypt, Moses, the burning bush, I AM, the plagues, the Passover, deliverance from Egypt, and provision in the desert).

Explain that after about three months in the desert, things were still a little up and down (no pun intended) with the Israelites. The people were learning to trust in God, but it was a very slow process: for every two steps they took forward, they seemed to take one step back. They needed some help, so they camped at the base of Mount Sinai, which is near the southern tip of the Sinai Peninsula, and Moses went to talk to God about what to do next.

Hand out Bibles and have a volunteer read aloud Exodus 19:3-6. Comment that God began by reminding Moses of the way that He had rescued the Israelites. That rescue proved not only God's great love for the people but also His great power. Verse 4 uses the picture of God as an eagle carrying His people on His wings up to a safe place. God chose them. God redeemed them. It was His idea. Their rescue was not based on anything they did.

This is important to emphasize because it sets the stage for our New Testament understanding of grace. Just like the Israelites, we cannot earn God's love or His powerful deliverance. It was and is His idea from start to finish. And based on this relationship, God wants His people to commit to obedience. Reread aloud verses 5-6. God was very clear that He wanted to have a unique relationship with the Israelites. Even though the whole world belongs to Him, He had chosen them to share life with in a unique way. Note, however, that it was through this special relationship that God's blessing would eventually extend to all people.

Have a volunteer read aloud Exodus 19:7-8. Comment that the people said a resounding yes to God's revelation. He had redeemed them and they were His. They said that they would obey Him and do whatever He tells them. Thus, His words, His commandments, are rooted in the special relationship He had initiated with them (and with us).

Since they agreed to His plan, God explained that *He would come down* to Mount Sinai and, through Moses, He would reveal His will to the people. That God would come down is also an important point to emphasize, because it is another glimpse into the gospel of grace. Jesus came down for us!

Summarize Exodus 19:9-15 for the group: The Israelites took three days to prepare to be in God's presence. This lets us know that it wasn't a casual, easygoing picnic—not because God was being overly pretentious, but because He is completely holy. He wasn't a guy from some desert oasis, meeting up for some figs and honey. Being in His presence called for utmost respect and reverence. To this end, the people would be able to be near the mountain, but they were told not to step on it or to even touch it.

Have a volunteer read aloud Exodus 19:16-21. As the passage is read, flip up and down the light switch in your meeting space and start to play the thun-

OLD WEST CHARACTERS

TEDDY ROOSEVELT (1858–1919)

Theodore Roosevelt was a naturalist, explorer, hunter, author, soldier and the twenty-sixth President of the United States. Born into a wealthy family, "Teddy" was a sickly child who suffered from asthma, so to compensate he engaged in strenuous outdoor activities. In 1898 he formed a volunteer calvary unit called "the Rough Riders" and became a hero during the Spanish-American War fought that same year. After becoming President at age 42, he was a force for conservationism and established numerous National Parks and National Forests across the United States. The well-known "Teddy Bear" was named after him.

der sound effect. Then play the sound effect for the trumpet blast. Invite group members to think about the phenomena that occurred when God came down to Mount Sinai: thunder, lightning, clouds, trumpet blast, smoke and fire, and earthquakes. Guide the group to see that even nature recognized the greatness of God. His power and His presence were overwhelming. It should have been clear to the people that they would need to live a different kind of life in order to pursue a relationship with God. This experience emphasized to the Israelites the holiness of God, which served as a backdrop for the holiness to which He would call His people.

Then God gave the Ten Commandments to Moses to give to His people so that they would have the basis for living better lives, holy lives.

As you read aloud each commandment (Exodus 20:1-17), have a volunteer turn over the appropriate poster at the front of your meeting space. (Add some drama by flipping the light switch and playing the thunder sound effect after each commandment is read.) Invite group members to sum up in their own words what each commandment means.

1. Exodus 20:1-3—There is only one true God, and we are not to have any other gods.

2. Exodus 20:4-6—We cannot worship anything besides God. He demands wholehearted devotion.

3. Exodus 20:7—God's name is more than a label; it is an expression of His nature. We must revere His name as we do His very presence.

4. Exodus 20:8-11—Keeping a day of rest and worship reminds us of two things: (1) God cares about every aspect of our lives and knows that we need to rest, and (2) God is an essential part of our lives. We must regularly stop our busyness for our good health, and we must spend time worshiping God, instead of staying focused on our lives and our pursuits.

5. Exodus 20:12—Our parents are God-given authorities over our lives. When we honor them, we honor God.

6. Exodus 20:13—We must not willingly take away life from other people.

7. Exodus 20:14—We must not break marriage promises.

8. Exodus 20:15—We must not take what isn't ours.

9. Exodus 20:16—We must not lie or shade the truth, even a little.

10. Exodus 20:17—We must not get jealous about the things other people have.

Suggest to the group that in the Old West, cowboys had what became known as the Code of the West, which were unwritten rules of behavior the cowboys could expect every other cowboy to follow. Because of these unwritten rules, cowboys knew how they and the people around them should conduct themselves. The Ten Commandments are God's rules of conduct—a "God Code," so to speak—so we know how to live God's way and how we can expect others to live.

Invite volunteers to tell how the Ten Commandments help people lead better lives. Remind the group that God gave us rules not to confine us but to guide us. The Ten Commandments showed the Israelites—and us—how to live redeemed lives well.

DIG

Live *for* Him. For this activity, you'll need Bibles and the posters from the Message segment of this session. Tape the posters, commandments facing out, to the front of your meeting space.

Invite group members to consider how they might divide the Ten Commandments into two separate groups. Guide them to see that the first four commandments are about their interaction with God and the last six are about their interaction with people. (Some Jewish teachings hold that "honor your parents" is actually better placed with the first four commandments, because parents are the biological creators of children and have a relationship to each other that is similar to that between God and humankind. Parents may also be considered an extension of God's authority and are thus also deserving of respect. That would make the first five commandments about submission to God and the second five about service to humankind.)

Pass out Bibles. Explain that Jesus helped bring together this division of the Ten Commandments during His conversation with a teacher of the law. Have a volunteer read Mark 12:28-31. The Ten Commandments can be summed up in two parts: love God and love others. Point out to the group that despite what they might think, love is the goal of the commandments. Review the commandments, and as you read each one, invite a volunteer to tell how doing that commandment demonstrates love. Then have another volunteer read aloud John 13:34-35. Explain that Jesus was not giving us a "new" commandment but was giving a summary of the last six command-ments, and He was also saying that when we show love, we show that we are His followers. In other words, love is the earmark of a true believer.

The idea that obedience to God's command is a result of love for Him and for others is repeated throughout the New Testament. Have different volun-teers read aloud the following verses and help the group see the connection between love and obedience:

- John 14:15
- John 14:24
- 1 John 2:5
- 1 John 4:20-21
- 1 John 5:3

When God brought His people out of bondage in Egypt, He knew that they would need help learning how to live well, so He gave them the Ten Com-mandments. By following these rules of conduct, by using this sort of God Code, the Israelites could conduct their lives in such a way that they would be-come more holy and be blessed by God. Those Ten Commandments were then summed up in Jesus' two: love God and love others (see Matthew 22:37-39; Mark 12:29-31). And those two can be reduced to one word: "love." That's it! When we obey the command to love, we are letting God direct our hearts to-ward His ultimate redemptive purpose for us.

APPLY

Move to Him. For this activity, you'll need a set of horse reins; staplers; and for each group member a 6"x 8" piece of heavy fabric, a marker, a piece of thick yarn about 3 yards long, and a piece of thick yarn about 14-inches long.

Hold up the reins and explain that cowboys use reins to guide their horses, enabling them to follow their lead with confidence. With the reins, a rider can signal the horse to slow down, speed up, turn and stop, among other maneu-vers. In a similar way, the commandments God gave us are like reins that en-able us to follow Him with confidence. Jesus said that His commands are not burdensome; instead, they direct us on how to live better lives.

Have group members make a reminder of the "reins" of God's Word by cre-ating a set of yarn reins for themselves (have any helpers you have make reins for themselves and make some for yourself). Give each person a piece of fabric, a marker and two lengths of yarn. On the fabric, have group members write, "God's commands lead my life." Tie a knot at each end of each piece of yarn.

Then, to each top corner of the 8-inch length of fabric, group members will staple one end of the shorter piece of yarn (to go over the head and hold the fabric across the chest—the knot will keep the yarn from pulling out of the staple). Next, to each bottom corner of the 8-inch length of fabric, group members will staple one end of the longer piece of yarn (to go behind the person and act as reins with which to guide him or her). Have group members (and you and your helpers) wear reins and take turns using each others' reins to direct each other along an imaginary path.

This will give everyone a chance to feel how reins work and to connect them with the idea that God's Commandments do the same thing for us on several different levels (physical, emotional, mental and spiritual): His Words direct our lives toward blessings and fulfillment. End the session by praying for the group, asking God to help the group obey His commands.

REFLECT

Be *with* **Him.** The following short devotions are for group members to reflect on and answer during the week. You can make copies of these pages and distribute them to your group members, or you can download and print the pages from **www.gospellight.com/uncommon/jh_Jesus_is_with_me.zip.**

1—COMMANDED TO BELIEVE

Read 1 John 3:23. The two commands in this verse summarize the two sections into which the Ten Commandments can be divided, which are the same two things Jesus told the teacher in Mark 12:28-31: We need to keep our relationship with God in a good place, and we need to keep our relationships with others in a good place. Notice that the relationship to God always comes first. Why do you think that is the case?

_____

_____

_____

_____

How would you describe your relationship to God right now? What could you do to strengthen it?

_____

_____

_____

How would you describe your relationships with family members and friends right now? What could you do to show them God's love today?

_____

_____

_____

Take a minute to ask God to help you have better relationships with Him and with your family members and friends. Work to strengthen those relationships!

2—DEFINED BY LOVE

Think about the most defining aspect of your character. In other words, when people think of you, what traits probably come to mind?

_____

_____

_____

Jesus said that the most defining characteristic of His disciples is love. Look up 1 Corinthians 13:4-7 and list all the things love is and isn't.

_____

_____

_____

Circle two things that love is that are easy for you to do. Underline two that are hard for you to do. Now reread the passage, and instead of saying "love," say your own name. How does that change how you think about yourself?

_____

_____

_____

3—HELPED BY THE HOLY SPIRIT

Read Romans 5:1-5. When we first believed in Jesus, what did God do?

_____

_____

_____

Read 1 John 4:8. Why is what God did when we first believed more than just a feeling, or an emotion?

_____

_____

_____

How does knowing that God is in you make you feel about how you talk and act?

_____

_____

_____

Take a minute and thank God for the help His Holy Spirit gives us to live a life of obedience and love.

4—LED BY EXAMPLE

Read John 15:9-12. Jesus tells us to *stay* in His love. According to verse 10, how do we stay in His love?

_____

_____

_____

According to verse 11, what emotion comes from loving obedience?

_____

_____

_____

Take a minute to say a prayer asking God to help you show your love for Him by obeying His command to love others.

ULTIMATE COURAGE

THE BIG IDEA

God will guide us through every trial we face.

SESSION AIMS

In this session, group members will learn that (1) God was in control of Joseph's life and was always with him, (2) God directs the course of our lives, and (3) we can rely on the guidance of Jesus, even when life is difficult.

THE BIGGEST VERSES

"God is our refuge and strength, an ever-present help in trouble. Therefore we will not fear, though the earth give way and the mountains fall into the heart of the sea" (Psalm 46:1-2).

OTHER IMPORTANT VERSES

Genesis 37; 39; Psalm 37:40; Proverbs 16:33; 19:21; Isaiah 46:10; Matthew 26:36-39; Luke 22:39-42; 1 Peter 4:19

People who settled in the Old West faced a number of difficulties, but one unexpected challenge was a series of earthquakes that leveled buildings and left visible fissures in newly built streets. In 1812, "Southern California was subject to nearly continuous earthquake shocks for four and one-half months. Four days seldom elapsed without at least one shock. The inhabitants abandoned their homes and lived out of doors."[1]

In 1857, an earthquake that was felt for as long as four minutes in San Francisco "cracked open the earth for 20 miles at Fort Tejon in lower California, knocked down all buildings there, and caused water in Mokolemne River to be thrown from its banks."[2] One eyewitness in San Francisco wrote that "brick walls were cracked, a small house which stood up on stilts was thrown down, and many people were much frightened, and ran out into the streets."[3]

Despite this, the settlers' response was not to give up and move back East. Instead, "These small shakings seem to be becoming fashionable in this particular portion of Uncle Sam's dominions, but as they do little or no damage, they are not much to be feared."[4] I don't know about you, but collapsed buildings and cracks in the earth seem like a lot more than "little or no damage"!

As followers of Jesus, we will no doubt face days when our problems and troubles seem so great that the very earth feels like it is quaking and falling out from under us. But like the Old West settlers, we can get back up and keep on going when we realize that God has everything—even moving ground—under control. There are no circumstances over which He is not sovereignly directing the outcome, through which He is not perfectly working out His will: "God is our refuge and strength, an ever-present help in trouble. Therefore, we will not fear, though the earth give way and the mountains fall into the heart of the sea" (Psalm 46:1-2).

When we maintain our faith and turn to God in both good times and bad, He will be with us and will guide us through every challenge we face.

STARTER

Depend *on* **Him.** For this activity, you need pieces of paper and pens or pencils.

Welcome the group, and explain the problems with a slippery slope argument, which assumes that one mildly unpleasant circumstance is linked to a series of increasingly unfortunate events that end in a major disaster. For example, if you don't do your homework, you'll end up homeless with nothing to eat and no one to love. The slippery slope scenario would go something like this: If you don't do your homework, you won't pass the class. If you don't pass the class, you won't graduate from school. If you don't graduate from school, you'll never get a good job. If you don't get a good job, you'll end up homeless, shivering alone in a deserted warehouse with nothing to eat and no one to love.

Divide the group into trios and give each trio a piece of paper and a pen or pencil. Instruct each group to write down a slippery slope scenario that tells how a cowboy with an ornery horse eventually ends up in jail. (If groups have trouble getting started, suggest a couple of possible ways to start: the ornery horse throws the cowboy who ends up hurt and in need of a doctor; or the ornery horse causes the cowboy to yell at another cowboy for no reason.) After several minutes, call the group members back together, and have a couple of volunteers tell their group's scenario.

Then tell the group that today's session is about the life of Joseph, which sounds like a slippery slope scenario—except it really happened! If Joseph's life were presented as a slippery slope scenario, it might sound like this: If your dad likes you, he will give you a colorful coat. If you wear a colorful coat, your siblings will hate you. If they hate you, they will attack you and throw you into a hole. If they throw you into a hole, you will be sold to a caravan of traders who will sell you to a highly placed government official whose wife will falsely accuse you of a crime, and you will end up all alone in the king's prison.

Point out that there are no slippery slope arguments or scenarios in God's kingdom. Circumstances do not control our future. God directs the course of our lives, so we can always rely on Him, even when things are difficult.

MESSAGE

Learn *from* Him. For this activity, you'll need Bibles, a colorful coat you won't mind ruining, a table, newspaper, scissors, red paint, a paintbrush, and a small container filled with dirt. Ahead of time, cover the table with newspaper.

Tell the group that the life of Joseph has many lessons for us to learn. Today we will be focusing on Genesis 37 and 39, which tell how Joseph went from favored son to deprived prisoner. And what we want to look at today is that despite the seeming disaster, God's power was always at work, bringing about His perfect will. Just like Joseph, we can rely on God, even when life is difficult.

Hand out Bibles and ask the group to follow along while a volunteer reads aloud Genesis 37:1-11. Note that one of the reasons Joseph was favored over his other brothers was the fact that he was the son of Jacob's favorite wife, Rachel (see Genesis 30:22-24), and it had taken them many years to have a child. Joseph's brothers were the sons of Jacob's other wives.

Invite a few volunteers to tell why Joseph's older brothers did not get along with him. Make sure they mention (1) Joseph's being something of a tattletale (maybe not on purpose—after all, his dad *had* sent him to check on his brothers); (2) the brothers' jealousy of how much Jacob loved Joseph, as evidenced by the gift of a coat; and (3) Joseph's dreams (the brothers [and Joseph's parents] would bow down to Joseph).

Point out that both the coat and the dreams were particularly significant because they were signs of Joseph's future as a ruler. Hold up the coat, and point out that the coat that Jacob had made for Joseph was "richly ornamented," as if for royalty (verse 3). In each of the two dreams Joseph had, his family bowed down before him. Both things incited hatred in the brothers and the second a rebuke from Jacob, but they suggested the future God intended for Joseph: God would place him in a position of authority.

Have another volunteer read aloud Genesis 37:12-24 and another volunteer read aloud Genesis 37:25-36. Invite a volunteer or two to sum up how Joseph ended up in Egypt. As the basics are recapped, hold up the coat over the prepared table, make a few cuts in it with the scissors and brush the coat with some red paint to symbolize the brothers' attempt to cover up their sin by making it look as if a wild animal had eaten Joseph. Explain that Joseph must have felt as if the ground beneath his feet was quaking and throwing his life in turmoil. Things just kept going from bad to worse, and the slippery slope was just beginning.

OLD WEST CHARACTERS

ANNIE OAKLEY (1860–1926)

"Annie Oakley" the stage name for Phoebe Ann Moses, was a sharpshooter and exhibition shooter. Born in a cabin in Ohio, she began shooting at the age of eight to support her family. By 1885 her reputation in the region had grown to the point where she was asked to join Buffalo Bill's Wild West Show, where she performed tricks such as splitting a playing card in half and shooting more holes into it before it hit the ground. In 1902 she quit the show and took up acting, though she continued to set records into her sixties. After an auto accident in 1922 her health steadily declined, and she died in 1926.

Photo: Unknown (c. 1880s). Public domain.

Have another volunteer read aloud Genesis 39:1-10 and another volunteer read aloud Genesis 39:11-23. Invite different volunteers to recap the basics of the story, and as they do, take the paint-stained coat and rub some dirt into it to suggest what Joseph's clothes would have looked like in prison. Point out that just when Joseph's life seemed to be settled, the quaking came again, and he ended up farther down the slippery slope and in a prison cell!

Invite the group members to look carefully at the paint-stained, dirt-encrusted, cut-up coat. Explain that it might seem as if the promising future God seemed to have planned for Joseph had been effectively—and permanently—knocked down. The brothers had "stripped him of his robe . . . and they took him and threw him into the cistern" (Genesis 37:23-24). Potiphar "took him and put him in prison" (Genesis 39:20). But none of this mattered, because God was always with Joseph and gave him "success in everything he did" (Genesis 39:3; see also Genesis 39:23).

Explain that in the Old West, people refused to let little things like earthquakes stop them from pursuing their dreams. In the same way, Joseph never gave up his belief in God. Other people could take away Joseph's robe and his freedom but not his faith and his destiny. Joseph never really touched the bottom of the slippery slope because circumstances and people can't stop God's blessings when we continue to trust in Him.

DIG

Live for Him. For this activity, you'll need Bibles, a copy of "Sometimes You Gotta Go Through It" (found on the next two pages) for every group member, and pens or pencils.

Remind the group that there is a unique relationship between the Old and New Testaments. From a Christian perspective, the Old Testament is not only a narrative of God's interactions with the Israelites but also a picture of God's plan to save humankind. The life of Joseph provides us with a good example of a courageous man who trusted God in every difficult situation with which he had to deal. But Joseph foreshadows a much better example of having the courage to trust God: Jesus Christ. Like Joseph, Jesus was betrayed by his brothers (His fellow Jews) and was passed from one group of people (the chief priests and the Sanhedrin) to a single person (Pilate). And like Joseph, Jesus was accused of a crime He did not commit and was imprisoned. Unlike Joseph, Jesus knew that the trial was part of God's plan of salvation and that He must walk through the pain to get the blessing.

Sometimes You've Gotta Go Through It

It would be great if we could wave a magic wand and never experience any difficulty, wouldn't it? If we could somehow skip past every unpleasant, awkward or painful situation? Or would that really be such a great thing?

Read Mark 14:32-36. What was Jesus doing in Gethsemane?

_____
_____
_____
_____

How did Jesus feel at the time?

_____
_____
_____
_____

What did Jesus ask His Father to do?

_____
_____
_____
_____

Why do you think Jesus asked His disciples to "keep watch"?

_____
_____
_____
_____

Why is companionship important during a difficult time?

_____
_____
_____
_____

How well did the disciples keep watch?

_____
_____
_____
_____

Read Hebrews 12:2-3. Why did Jesus endure the cross?

_____
_____
_____
_____

What would have happened if Jesus had given up?

_____
_____
_____
_____

Why should what Jesus did inspire faith in us?

_____
_____
_____
_____

What are a few specific things you can do to show that you model Jesus' behavior of courage in difficulty?

_____
_____
_____
_____

Like it or not, it seems as if God uses difficult times to build up our faith in Him. Without those opportunities to trust Him, we would never grow to understand just how powerful and good He really is.

_____
_____
_____
_____

Hand out Bibles, copies of "Sometimes You Gotta Go Through It," and pens or pencils. Have pairs work together to answer the questions. Walk around and help anyone who appears to be stumped. Then gather everyone together. Have a volunteer read aloud Mark 14:32-36 and then invite volunteers to tell their answers to the questions on the handout. Follow the same procedure to discuss Hebrews 12:2-3. After you've discussed the responses of the group members, remind the group that just as Joseph and Jesus had the courage and faith to deal with every difficult situation they faced, we too have to have faith that God is in control and will help us meet and guide us through every difficult challenge and situation that we face.

APPLY

Move *to* Him. For this activity, you'll need Bibles bookmarked at the following verses: Exodus 15:2-3; Deuteronomy 33:29; 2 Samuel 22:3; Psalms 27:1; 46:1-2. You'll also need watercolors, paintbrushes, water, paper and tape.

Encourage the group members to think about what happened to Joseph: Everything that had been a firm foundation was shaken out from under him. However, no difficulty was able to diminish his faith in God. Joseph continued to trust and, as a result, the family trouble that led to his slavery also led to his ruling Potiphar's house. And the trouble that led to a jail cell also led to ruling the whole prison. And though Joseph could have rightfully cried out about the injustices he had suffered, he chose instead to trust God and to continue to obey Him. This is the key to walking through a difficult time!

Encourage the group to think about Jesus' example: He willingly faced an excruciating and unjust death in order to make a way for us to have a relationship with God. What Jesus did was difficult, He had to do it alone, and it literally cost Him His life—but He had faith in God's power and, as such, He provided us with an unparalleled example of how we should meet every challenging situation, every difficulty, and every problem we face.

Hand out Bibles. Read aloud Psalm 46:1-2. Point out that even when it seems as if the ground is trembling beneath our feet and at any moment might give way underneath us, we can have complete confidence in God's plan. Because God is in total control, we do not have to be afraid, and because God is always there to help us, we do not have to be afraid. We can have courage because with God at our side we can meet everything that comes our way.

Have volunteers read aloud the other verses you've marked in the Bibles. Invite group members to point out the objects to which God is compared. Then hand out the watercolors, paintbrushes, water and paper and invite each group member to paint a picture of the thing to which God is compared that means the most to him or her. Let the group know that you are more interested in their interpretation, not specific details.

After everyone is finished, tape the papers together to make one giant quilt of how God helps us through our difficulties. Display it in your meeting space or a hallway to remind the group that even if the ground trembles and falls away, those who trust in God will rise again. This is not because of their own strength or talent or goodness, but because God is with them to guide them and see them through life, even when life is difficult.

End the session by praying for the group, thanking God for being with everyone to guide them through every difficulty that they face in life.

REFLECT

Be *with* Him. The following short devotions are for group members to reflect on and answer during the week. You can make copies of these pages and distribute them to your group members, or you can download and print the pages from **www.gospellight.com/uncommon/jh_Jesus_is_with_me.zip.**

1—A HELP DURING DIFFICULTIES

Read Psalm 46. Yep, the whole thing. What are some of the negative things going on (see verses 2,3,6)?

_____

_____

_____

_____

What is the psalmist's response (see verse 2), and why can the psalmist respond this way (see verses 1-2,5,7,9,11)?

_____

_____

_____

_____

What does God say about Himself that is reassuring to the psalmist and to us (see verse 10)?

_____

_____

_____

_____

Write out a prayer thanking God that He is with you today, guiding you, helping you in times of trouble and working everything out by His power.

DAY 2—MIGHTY IN POWER

Read Isaiah 40:25-31. What did God do that makes Him worthy of our faith?

_____

_____

_____

_____

What will God do for those who put their faith in Him (see verses 29-31)?

_____

_____

_____

_____

_____

Oddly enough, it's really easy to forget just how powerful God really is. (Crazy, right?!) Look back through the passage and write down at least three names or characteristics of God.

_____

_____

_____

_____

Spend a minute praying to God and thanking Him for sharing His power with you. And the next time you gaze at a starry sky, remember that He knows each star by name, and if God can keep track of the stars, He can certainly watch over your life. Cool, huh?

DAY 3—ALWAYS WORTHY OF PRAISE

Read Acts 16:16-34. It's an interesting story—you'll like it. What happened to Paul and Silas, and why did it happen (see verses 19-24)?

_____

_____

_____

_____

What did Paul and Silas do while they were in jail, and what two groups of people did they influence (see verses 25,28,31-33)?

_____

_____

_____

_____

_____

When you have a difficulty in life, why is how you react so important for yourself and for others?

_____

_____

_____

_____

_____

Spend a minute in prayer, committing yourself to your faithful Creator and asking for His help to be a good influence on others.

DAY 4—PROVIDER OF EVERY PEACE

Read 2 Timothy 3:10-16. Why was Paul able to have courage and face the many trials he had during his life?

_____

_____

_____

_____

God's Word provided Paul with the same things with which it can provide us.
What are those things (see verses 15-16)?

_____

_____

_____

_____

Look up Psalm 119:11,92-93,130,165. What are the benefits that God's Word
can bring to your life, especially when you face hard times?

_____

_____

_____

_____

_____

Spend a minute reading and then praying Psalm 119:105-112. Then remember to spend a part of every day alone with God, reading His Word.

ULTIMATE ENCOURAGEMENT

THE BIG IDEA
God is our encouragement to stand firm against temptation.

SESSION AIMS
In this session, group members will (1) learn that Joseph stayed true to his faith, no matter what; (2) realize that their faith in God enables them to stand firm; and (3) recognize that Jesus' example is an encouragement for us to be like Him.

THE BIGGEST VERSE
"No temptation has seized you except what is common to man. And God is faithful; he will not let you be tempted beyond what you can bear. But when you are tempted, he will also provide a way out, so that you can stand up under it" (1 Corinthians 10:13).

OTHER IMPORTANT VERSES
Genesis 40–41; Matthew 6:13; Luke 11:13; 2 Thessalonians 3:3; James 1:13-15; 4:7; 2 Peter 1:3

When Thomas Jefferson made the Louisiana Purchase in 1803, he doubled the size of the United States. But because much of the new land was un- known, Jefferson commissioned an expedition to find out what resources the land offered and find a water route across the United States. Lewis and Clark and the men who accompanied them packed the necessary supplies and set off on a journey of exploration and discovery. The maps made during the expedition helped spur settlement of the new land, and many people were inspired to exchange their familiar Eastern seaboard communities for the glorious potential awaiting them in the land beyond.

Unfortunately, not all of those who traveled west saw their dreams suc- ceed. Not all of the people who traveled to the West even made it to their des- tination. Many died from illness, others were killed by wild animals, others died accidently, and still others died as a result of poor planning.

Once on a homestead, things still were not easy: Clearing the land for farming or ranching was backbreaking work, and the people had to be on the constant lookout for rustlers and robbers. Sometimes there seemed to be little in the way of encouragement to keep settlers and ranchers from just giv- ing up and giving in to the temptation to despair and go back to "civilized" society. Those who "kept the faith" and stuck it out did eventually reap the blessings of the new land, but it took many years of patience and pain before that happened.

The lives of many people in the Bible similarly reflect the idea of not giv- ing up and giving in to temptation and eventually reaping blessings—espe- cially Joseph. His life seemed to be filled with many painful experiences, but each of the difficult times Joseph faced prepared him to take his place as sec- ond in command of the most powerful nation of his day. So, rather than give in to temptation, we, like Joseph, can consider every temptation a pathway to greater blessing—as long as we maintain our confidence in God's power.

In 1 Corinthians 10:13, Paul tells us that God will never allow us to be tempted beyond what we can bear. God gave us His Son, Jesus, as a perfect example we can follow. Jesus underwent the same things we do, but He never gave up, gave in or gave way to temptation.

STARTER

Depend *on* Him. For this activity, you'll need some individually wrapped pieces of candy and room to move. (Ahead of time, check to make sure that no one is allergic to the food you provide.)

Welcome the group, and then invite one volunteer to be Temptation. Temptation can bend and twist and reach out but must remain standing in one spot in the middle of an open space in your meeting place. Scatter the candy around Temptation's feet. Group members try to get as close as possible to Temptation in order to grab a piece of candy without getting tagged by Temptation. Group members who are tagged must take a seat. When most of the group has been tagged, have everyone rest a bit and enjoy the treat.

Explain to the group that every day we all face temptations to do things we know are wrong. Although God always provides us with a way to resist temptation, there are some things we can do to avoid being tempted at all. For example, flirting with temptation—coming close to doing something wrong without really doing it—is very dangerous. For a while you may be able to resist it, but at some point you're bound to be caught by temptation and give in to it. And you end up committing a sin.

MESSAGE

Learn *from* Him. For this activity, you'll need Bibles. Begin by asking group members to tell things they recall about Joseph. In spite of the difficult times he went through, he never gave in to temptation and did anything wrong. And because he was faithful to God, God blessed him and he prospered.

Briefly describe that when settlers began to move to the West after Lewis and Clark had explored the new land that President Jefferson had purchased, they were lured by the great expanses of land, the possibilities they imagined, and the dreams they thought they could fulfill. They gave up the safety and security of "civilized" society and ventured west, but not all of them succeeded.

Many gave in to despair and gave up their dreams. They "lost faith," maybe discouraged by the hardship of travel itself, by the back-breaking work it took to clear the land, by encounters with robbers or rustlers, or even by wild animals with which they had had no previous experience. Giving in to the temptation to despair of their situation and to go back where they had come from must have tempted even the most determined souls. Dealing with temptation is never all that easy. And the story of Joseph in the Bible is a great example.

Hand out Bibles, and invite volunteers to read aloud the parts of Joseph, the cupbearer and the baker while you read aloud the narration of Genesis 40. Invite group members to identify from this chapter evidence that Joseph had not been discouraged by his time in prison, that he had kept his faith in God and that he continued to do what was right in spite of probably being tempted to complain or despair (Joseph showed that he cared about his fellow prisoners; Joseph told the cupbearer and the baker that God can explain dreams and will do so if asked; Joseph interpreted the dreams of the cupbearer and the baker).

Invite new volunteers to read aloud the parts of Pharaoh, the cupbearer and Joseph as you continue to read aloud the narration, now for Genesis 41. Again invite group members to identify evidence that indicates Joseph's continued faith in God and his resistance to the temptation to despair or complain about his situation. (It had been *two years* since Joseph helped the cupbearer, yet Joseph was still in prison. The cupbearer remembered him and was able to recommend him to Pharaoh. Joseph admitted he could not interpret dreams but that God could. Joseph told Pharaoh what his dreams meant.)

Continue by stating that Joseph maintained his faith and confidence in God and His power. And Joseph again had success in what he was given to do, this time as Pharaoh's second in command. Joseph was also given a wife, and the names he gave his first two sons also reflect his faith in God: One son was named Manasseh "because God has made me forget all my trouble and all my father's household" and the other son was named Ephraim "because God has made me fruitful in the land of my suffering" (Genesis 41:51-52). Yes, it is true that Joseph had suffered and had been tempted, but God hadn't given him anything that he couldn't bear. Joseph had continued to do what was right in God's sight.

OLD WEST CHARACTERS

RED CLOUD (1822–1909)

Maȟpíya Lúta was chief of the Oglala Lakota (Sioux) from 1868 to 1909. He led a series of successful campaigns against the U.S. Army from 1866 to 1868, prompting troops to refer to the conflict as "Red Cloud's War." Following the battle, a peace commission met with the Plains tribes and agreed to assign specific territories to them. The U.S. also agreed to abandon its forts and forces from Lakota territory. In later life, Red Cloud became an important leader as the Lakotas transitioned from freedom to the confinement of the reservation system. He died still fighting for his people at the age of 87.

Photo: South Dakota State Historical Society. Public domain.

DIG

Live *for* Him. For this activity, you'll need Bibles, a copy of "Temptation Tests" (found on the next page) for every group member, and pens or pencils.

Explain to the group that shortly after His baptism, Jesus went to the desert, where Satan tempted Him. Hand out Bibles, copies of "Temptation Tests," and pens or pencils. Have pairs work together to complete the handout. Then gather the group members back together and first review their responses to the questions about the Bible passage. Make sure the group members understand that although Jesus is God, He became a man. And because Jesus became a man, He was subject to all of the same things with which we have to deal. Because Jesus never gave in to temptation, He is the One whose behavior we should model.

Then go over the last three questions on the handout, inviting volunteers to tell their ideas. Emphasize with the group that no matter how hard our situations may be, we really have no excuse for sinning, no matter how much we try to rationalize bad behavior. We always have a choice about what we do. This also applies to going along with friends who want to do something they know isn't right.

Make sure to get across the idea that one of the things the group members could do when they are tempted to follow the lead of someone to do wrong is suggest doing a different activity. If such a situation happens often enough, though, point out to the group that they may have to consider getting a new set of friends. In order to know what God wants them to do, they could, among other things, read and study the Bible, pray to God, spend time with Christian friends, and/or talk with an older and more mature Christian.

APPLY

Move *to* Him. For this activity, you'll need Bibles; several objects that represent different people, places and things in the lives of the group members (such as a magazine photo of a house to represent family, a small book to represent school, a friendship bracelet to represent friends, or a picture of a keyboard to represent the Internet); small bricks; tape; and string. Ahead of time, tape or tie the objects to the bricks.

Read aloud 1 Corinthians 10:13. Point out that "can" in this verse is translated from the Greek word *dynamai,* which means "to be capable, strong and powerful."[1] The phrase "stand up under it" is translated from the Greek word *hypophero,* which means "to bear under, to bear up under; to endure patiently."[2]

TEMPTATION TESTS

Remember that although He was God, Jesus became a man. And as a man, Jesus was subject to the same things that we are, including sore feet, the hot sun, angry parents—and temptation to sin. Read Matthew 4:1-11. Who led Jesus into the desert? Why did He go there (see verse 1)?

_____

_____

_____

How long had Jesus fasted (see verse 2)? _____

What were the three temptations (see verses 3,6,9)?

_____

_____

_____

With what did Jesus respond to every temptation? _____

What did Satan finally end up doing (see verse 11)?

_____

_____

_____

So Jesus faced temptations just like we do—actually maybe way harder than we do. But He didn't cave. Instead, He continued to obey the Word of God, even quoting it to keep the record straight. How might being in a difficult situation tempt us to rationalize disobedience?

_____

_____

_____

What can you do when you are tempted to go with friends to see a movie or play a video game that you know goes against what God says is right?

_____

_____

_____

This means that God promises that we have the capability, the strength and the power we need to bear up under the weight of any temptation that comes our way. In other words, we never have to give up or give in, because we will never face a temptation that we can't find the power to endure or bear. And what's really great is that God also provides a way out of every temptation.

Invite a volunteer to hold one of the bricks. Then invite another volunteer to tell a situation when someone might be tempted to do something wrong with those people, in that place or with that thing represented by what is attached to the brick. (If group members have trouble suggesting scenarios, be prepared to offer a few, such as a parent tells you to do a chore when you're in the middle of chatting with a friend; you are unprepared for a test and a friend offers to lend you his cheat sheet; your friend's parents aren't around, so she suggests you watch an X-rated movie; you're watching a music video and the song contains bad language; and so forth.) Have another volunteer tell a way out of the temptation. The volunteer holding the brick should not give in to the temptation to put it down before the temptation and way out can be described. Then have a different volunteer choose a different brick to hold, and repeat the process.

Remind the group that in 1 Corinthians 10:13, Paul states that we will never face trials we can't stand up under—if we remember that God is faithful. Point out to the group that a statement about God's character precedes the promise of endurance. God is faithful, which is what empowers us to bear up under temptation and avoid sinning. God will not allow the temptation to get so strong that a person must give in to it. Just like Joseph, though, we must learn to trust God when we're tempted to do wrong, so that we can become strong, full of godly character and ready to fulfill God's plan for our lives.

End the session by praying for the group, asking God to continue to encourage them to resist temptation and to help them be like Jesus, able to remember God's Word whenever they are tempted.

REFLECT

Be *with* Him. The following short devotions are for group members to reflect on and answer during the week. You can make copies of these pages and distribute them to your group members, or you can download and print the pages from **www.gospellight.com/uncommon/jh_Jesus_is_with_me.zip**.

1—ENCOURAGED BY ABRAHAM

The stories of the men and women in the Bible are not just cool tales of bravery (and sometimes stupidity!). They are meant to teach us how to live wisely and give us encouragement to face our own lives with hope. This week we'll be looking at a few people who did not give in to temptation, people who left us examples that can encourage us to do the same. Read Genesis 14. After winning a battle, Abraham was tempted by the king of Sodom to do what (see verse 21)?

_____

_____

_____

_____

If Abraham had done what the king wanted, what would Abraham have been obligated to do (see verse 23)?

_____

_____

_____

_____

How did Abraham show that his faith was only in God (see verses 22-23)?

_____

_____

_____

_____

Take a minute to pray and thank God that He gave us Bible stories of people who resisted the temptation to do wrong, and let God know if there is a particular temptation that you need help resisting.

2—ENCOURAGED BY SAMSON

Read Judges 13:5; 16. What was special about Samson, and what did Delilah tempt Samson to do (see Judges 13:5; 16:6,10,13)?

_____

_____

_____

_____

What was the result of Samson's giving in to Delilah's temptation?

_____
_____
_____
_____
_____

What did Samson do that showed that he still had faith in God and was literally able to stand firm (see Judges 16:28-30)?

_____
_____
_____
_____
_____
_____

Take a minute and thank God for the strength He has given you to resist any temptation that comes your way.

3—ENCOURAGED BY JOB

Read Job 1–2:10; 42:1-17. Job suffered more pain than perhaps anyone else in the Old Testament: He lost his children, home, resources, health and friends—all in a day or two. Who caused Job's situation and tempted him to sin?

_____
_____
_____
_____
_____

Even though he was probably tempted to give in to despair and lose his faith in God, how did Job respond to his change in circumstance (see Job 1:20)?

_____
_____
_____
_____
_____

Temptations and difficult circumstances don't become easier because we trust God, but they do become bearable. Job recognized this and continued to have faith in God. Read Job 42. What was Job's life like in the end?

_____

_____

_____

_____

Take a minute and say a prayer praising God for being there with you to encourage you to resist temptation.

4—ENCOURAGED BY JESUS

Read 1 Peter 2:21-24. When Jesus was tempted to complain about His fate after He was arrested, what did He do?

_____

_____

_____

_____

Read Hebrews 4:14-16. Why is Jesus our best model of standing firm against temptation?

_____

_____

_____

_____

What will Jesus give us when we call on Him when we need help?

_____

_____

_____

_____

Take a minute and say a prayer of thanksgiving for God's encouragement and faithfulness. Thank Him for giving us Jesus to save us and serve as our model of how to live.

ULTIMATE ABUNDANCE

THE BIG IDEA

God blesses us with abundance so that we can bless others.

SESSION AIMS

In this session, group members will (1) consider the way God's abundant blessing of Joseph enabled Joseph to be a blessing to others, (2) realize that God provides more than enough for us in any situation, and (3) understand that Jesus' abundant provision for us is meant to be shared with others.

THE BIGGEST VERSE

"But seek first his kingdom and his righteousness, and all these things will be given to you as well" (Matthew 6:33).

OTHER IMPORTANT VERSES

Genesis 42–47; 50:15-21; Exodus 34:6; Psalm 36:8-9; Malachi 3:10; Luke 5:1-11; 1 Corinthians 1:3-7

Hospitality was part of the Code of the West (discussed in session 5). Although there might not have been a lot of food available, whatever was available was shared. Anyone who rode into a trail camp, for example, was welcomed and invited to eat and have a cup of coffee, a pot of which was usually kept going on the coals. Anyone who rode into a ranch was usually invited to share whatever meal was being cooked.

A cowboy would share whatever he could, because there was always a chance that somewhere down the trail, he might need the same sort of help that he was able to provide to someone else. "Abundance" would not be a word that would accurately describe the resources available to a cowboy, but what he did have, he in effect used to bless others.

And that's one of the lessons we learn from the life of Joseph. Joseph did what was right and helped others as much as he could in whatever situation he found himself, and God granted him success—God blessed him and provided abundantly for him. In turn, Joseph was able to share his abundance—his blessings—with others. God wants us to do the same. Jesus provided for us by dying for our sins and making it possible for us to have eternal life, and He wants us to share this and our other blessings with others. Our lives are about more than ourselves.

STARTER

Depend on Him. For this activity, you'll need one large blanket for every six group members.

Welcome the group, and have them form groups of six. Explain that they've been invited to join the cowboys around the campfire and bed down for the night. Because the ground is super cold, the cowboys have provided each group with a blanket (aren't they nice!). Spread the blankets on the floor and invite each group of six to get on one blanket so that everyone is completely on it—no one can touch the floor at all.

Once the group is settled on the blanket, explain that you've received word that another half of their group blanket is needed by some other cowboys who just rode in. Ask them to get off the blanket, fold it in half and then get back on the blanket so that no one is touching the floor. Repeat this as many times as possible. Each time the groups fold their blankets, they will need to get everyone back on it completely.

Guide the group to see that we can take whatever we have been given and use it to be a blessing to others. Sometimes, though, we may have to make sacrifices to bless others. Sometimes you have to give up something—in this case, personal space and general comfort—in order to give to people what they need. Fortunately, God is generous with His abundance. Just as God provided great blessing out of Joseph's life, He will provide more than enough for us in any situation, and then we can share His blessing with others. We can use whatever we have been given wherever we are to be a blessing to other people.

MESSAGE

Learn *from* **Him.** For this activity, you'll need Bibles, a 10-foot length of butcher paper, tape and markers. Ahead of time, tape the paper to a wall where all group members will be able to clearly see it. Be prepared to draw stick figures to illustrate the rest of Joseph's story (Genesis 42–47; 50:15-21) as you or a helper tell the story in your own words or from a children's Bible storybook.

Invite group members to recap Joseph's life based on what they recall from the previous sessions (his fancy coat, his dreams, his brothers' rejection, his enslavement in Egypt, his unjust imprisonment, his interpretation of dreams, and his final elevation to a position of authority and esteem under Pharaoh). Draw attention to the fact that Joseph was 17 years old when his brothers sold him to the traders, and when Genesis 42 opens, Joseph was 39. Joseph hadn't seen his family for 22 years.

Tell the group to imagine what it would be like for them if tomorrow they were forced into slavery and could not see any family members (or anyone or anything else familiar) for 22 years. The main reason Joseph had success was because he remained faithful to God. No matter where Joseph was, God abundantly provided for him, and he had success. Just as He was with Joseph, so too God is always with us, working out everything for our good and His glory. Joseph never lost sight of the truth that God was with him. And through Joseph, God's blessings of abundance were extended to others.

Next, either summarize Genesis 42–47; 50:15-21 in your own words or read aloud from a children's Bible storybook, and draw at least one illustration for each of the main events from each chapter of Genesis. Make sure you make the following points:

- Genesis 42: Jacob sent 10 of his sons to Egypt to get grain. Joseph recognized them, demanded to see Benjamin, sent them home with their silver but kept Simeon in prison. (Hmm . . . unjust accusation and imprisonment. Sound familiar?)

- Genesis 43: Jacob sent the brothers back to Egypt and reluctantly agreed to let Benjamin go with them as well. Joseph held a feast for the brothers and sat them in birth order, giving Benjamin five times as much food as the others were given. (You'd think the brothers would start to get suspicious.)

- Genesis 44: Joseph set up Benjamin to look like a thief and demanded to keep him in Egypt as a slave. Judah stepped up and offered his own life instead—anything to free Benjamin and spare Jacob. (Finally! Someone who is willing to sacrifice to save his brother.)

- Genesis 45: Joseph dismissed his attendants and revealed himself to his brothers. He explained that his life had been steadily guided by God alone. They may have sold him, but it was God who sent him. Joseph wasn't angry. He told them to send for their families.

- Genesis 46: Jacob moved to Egypt with his entire family and everything he owned. Joseph was reunited with his family. Everyone was happy again.

- Genesis 47: Joseph settled his family in the land of Goshen, and Jacob blessed the pharaoh. Joseph even got some of his brothers jobs working for Pharaoh.

OLD WEST CHARACTERS

OLIVER WINCHESTER (1810–1880)

 Oliver Winchester is best known for manufacturing the Winchester repeating rifle, known as the "Gun that Won the West" because of its predominant role in the hands of early American settlers. He began his career as a clothing manufacturer in New York City, but when he learned that a division of Smith & Wesson firearms was failing, he invested in the company. Despite slow initial sales, the company made refinements until the gun became the most popular rifle in the country. Winchester was also active in politics, serving as lieutenant governor of Connecticut in 1864. He died at the age of 70 in 1880.

Photo: Unknown. Public domain.

- Genesis 50:15-21: After Jacob died, Joseph's brothers worried that Joseph would take revenge on them for what they had done to him when he was younger. Joseph, however, reassured his brothers that he had no such intention. In fact, he pointed out that what they had intended as harmful, "God intended . . . for good" (Genesis 50:20). God had arranged Joseph's life so that he would be able to save thousands of people from starvation and thus be a blessing for many people.

Once you've finished telling Joseph's story, read Genesis 45:5-8 and 50:20. Draw attention to the fact that Joseph recognized an important truth: A sovereign God governs our lives and shares His abundance with us, and He wants us to share that abundance with others.

Explain that the brothers had been worried that once their father died, Joseph would take revenge on them. However, Joseph wasn't interested in revenge because he saw his life not as a series of painful detours but as divine preparation for being able to bless many, many people. Because of his position in Egypt, Joseph was able to abundantly provide food for other people so that lives would be saved. Jesus abundantly provided for us by dying on the cross so that our lives would be saved for eternity. Such abundance deserves to be shared, and God expects us to share it.

DIG

Live *for* **Him.** For this activity, you'll need a whiteboard and erasable marker, or a flip chart and marker, and a rope.

Invite the group members to brainstorm a list of things with which God has blessed us. As volunteers tell ideas, list them on a whiteboard or flip chart. In addition to listing such physical things as ears to hear, eyes to see, and so on, make sure the group lists the obvious things that the group members might forget (such as water, air or sunlight) as well as intangible things (such as talents, skills or knowledge).

Have the group form a circle facing each other. Point out that in the Old West, people shared with others whatever they had, even though what they had may not have been much. The point was to share whatever existed in abundance, even a small "abundance."

Take the rope and, holding one end of it, throw the rest to a member of the group. As you do, tell something that you can use to bless someone else ("I'm good at reading, so I can read to someone who is in a hospital"). Then that person throws the rope to another person and tells what he or she could do to be a blessing to someone else (maybe, "I'm good at soccer, so I could help someone else learn the game" or "I'm good at singing, so I could entertain at a nursing home").

Continue until everyone's connected. Then point out that it is our belief in Jesus that is a blessing we can all share, something that connects us to each other and that we can share with more people so that one day, all people will be connected to God.

APPLY

Move *to* Him. For this activity, you'll need a Bible, and a whiteboard and erasable marker, or a flip chart and marker.

Invite volunteers to tell what is most important in their lives, what they spend the most time doing. As volunteers tell ideas, list them on the whiteboard or flip chart. Keep going until you have a pretty long list of things that occupy everyone's time and thoughts.

Then read aloud Matthew 6:33. Invite volunteers to tell what "seek first his kingdom and his righteousness" means. Make sure the group realizes that God's kingdom is not so much an actual place as it is an attitude and an action: We are to turn to God first for and in everything. We are to be like Joseph and seek only to obey and serve God.

Point out that the list the group made is actually a list of things that can distract us from what God wants us to do. It's not that we can't do those things or shouldn't do those things but that God wants to be first in everything we do. Invite volunteers to tell specific ways that they can actively seek God's righteousness. Make sure that the list includes praying to God, reading the Bible and hanging out with other Christians. Discuss how they can put God first while they do the activities in their day.

End the session by praying for the group, thanking God for His abundant blessings and asking help to share our blessings with others.

REFLECT

Be *with* Him. The following short devotions are for group members to reflect on and answer during the week. You can make copies of these pages and distribute them to your group members, or you can download and print the pages from **www.gospellight.com/uncommon/jh_Jesus_is_with_me.zip**.

1—ABUNDANCE WITHOUT LIMIT

Read James 1:17. From where does everything good—all abundance—come?

_____

_____

_____

_____

Now look at Ephesians 3:20. How did Paul describe God's abundance?

_____

_____

_____

_____

Take a minute to say a prayer thanking God for His limitless abundance and His goodness.

2—ABUNDANCE FROM THE BEGINNING

Read Genesis 1:11-13,20-29. How was God's abundance evident in how He created the universe?

_____

_____

_____

_____

Read Genesis 2:7. What did God do with His very breath?

_____

_____

_____

Now look at Genesis 3:14-15. What plan did God already have in mind after Adam and Eve sinned?

_____

_____

_____

_____

Take a minute to pray and thank God for the abundance with which He has provided you. Also be sure to thank Him for His promise to send Jesus to defeat Satan.

3—ABUNDANCE IN THE PAST

Skim through Exodus 16–17:7 (yes, this is the story you discussed in Session 4; that's why you should only need to skim through it!). With what did God abundantly provide the Israelites in the desert?

_____

_____

_____

_____

_____

Now read Deuteronomy 30:9-10. What did God promise to the Israelites when they were about to enter Canaan?

_____

_____

_____

_____

What was the condition that God imposed?

_____

_____

_____

_____

Read Joshua 1:3-5. How else did God plan to abundantly provide for the Israelites?

_____

_____

_____

_____

_____

Take a minute and thank God for fulfilling His promise to give abundantly to His people in the past and for His assurance that He still keeps His promises.

4—ABUNDANCE IN CHRIST

Read John 10:10. What did Jesus come to do for us?

_____

_____

_____

_____

_____

According to Philippians 4:19, how does God supply all that we need?

_____

_____

_____

_____

_____

What will we ultimately receive from God's abundance (see 2 Peter 1:11)?

_____

_____

_____

_____

Remember that what we want is not necessarily what we need, and it is what we need that God supplies from His abundance. Spend a minute asking God to help you recognize that what you want is not necessarily what you need. Then praise God for always providing from His abundance everything that you need.

ULTIMATE REDEMPTION

THE BIG IDEA

Remembering how God rescued the Israelites reminds us that Jesus rescues us.

SESSION AIMS

In this session, group members will (1) see the importance of remembering what God has done, (2) recall the roles Joseph and Moses played in how God intended to and then did redeem His Chosen People, and (3) recognize that God's intention and will to redeem us was fulfilled in Jesus.

THE BIGGEST VERSE

"Blessed is the one who perseveres under trial, because when he has stood the test, he will receive the crown of life that God has promised to those who love him" (James 1:12).

OTHER IMPORTANT VERSES

Psalm 105; Isaiah 40:9-11; 1 Corinthians 1:4-8; Philippians 4:13; 1 Timothy 2:5-6; Hebrews 11:6; Revelation 5:9

Sing to your cows, and they won't stampede. It's true. Cowboys used to offer their sweet voices throughout the night to keep their herds settled and calm. One man reported that he would ride on one side of the herd and sing a verse, and the other cowboy on guard would ride on the opposite side of the herd and respond with the next verse.[1]

The songs—including such favorites as "The Old Chisholm Trail," "Git Along, Little Dogies," "The Range of the Buffalo," "The Cowboy's Lament," and "I Ride an Old Paint"—covered a wide range of subjects, each touching on something personal or on the ranch or the trail.[2] And while the songs sung during guard duty at night calmed the cattle, the songs also kept the cowboys awake and let each other know where they were.

The songs were also sung around the campfire and while on the trail, partly for entertainment purposes. What's also interesting is that, generally speaking, there were "only three rhythms, all coming from the gaits of the cowpony—walk, trot, and lope."[3] Little if anything is known about the authors of most cowboy songs but somehow the composers managed to touch the heartstrings, not just of the cowboy, but also of a wider audience that still enjoys listening to cowboy songs today.

Songs have always been a vital part of culture for many reasons. They embody our hopes and dreams, express our fears and longings, tout our passions and aspirations, galvanize our thoughts and feelings. The Bible contains one of the best songbooks ever: the book of Psalms! This collection of 150 songs runs the gamut of expression—from praises to questions to rants. But each song voices a story of God's faithfulness and draws us closer to a life of faith and obedience leading to redemption and eternal life.

STARTER

Depend *on* Him. For this activity, you'll need old magazines, scissors, tape and 36 small index cards. From the magazines, cut two copies of the same 18 pictures (or print pictures from the Internet). Choose pictures that relate to the previous Bible stories or to the Old West. Then tape the pictures to the index cards. Ahead of time, arrange the cards facedown as in a game of Concentration (be sure to mix them up!). (If you have a large group, prepare two or more Concentration games.)

Welcome the group members, and then divide the group into two teams. Invite all group members to gather around the card grid you have laid out. Then have one member of one team turn over two cards. If the cards match, the player gets to keep them, and he or she takes another turn. If the cards don't match, the player replaces the cards facedown in the exact same spots, and a player from the other team tries to get a match. Play continues, alternating between the two teams and different players, until all of the pairs are matched. The winner is the team who has the most pairs.

Suggest to the group members that they think about their earliest memories. How do they know that their early memories are true? Often our most vibrant memories are not only things we have experienced but also things our families have talked about over and over again. Who hasn't attended a family gathering replete with conversations that start with "Remember the time you . . ." or "How about the day that . . ."? Every time someone retells a memory, it is reinforced in our minds and becomes a part of our thinking about our past and a suggestion about what the future may be like. Memories are important pieces of our heritage and our identity.

Explain that today the group will be taking a look at a song that is one long retelling of the way God rescued His people. The Israelites sang this song specifically so that they and their children and their grandchildren and their great-grandchildren would remember who they were: people God chose to save and love. This memory was fundamental to their identity. And it is fundamental for us as well, because just as God revealed His will and intentions for the Israelites and saved them, so too Jesus fulfilled God's will and intentions to redeem us.

MESSAGE

Learn *from* **Him.** You will need Bibles, paper, colored markers and a large photo album.

Hand out Bibles and explain that the book of Psalms contains a collection of songs that the Israelites sang—and many people today still sing!—about God's faithfulness and interactions with humanity. Like the songs cowboys on the prairies used to sing to calm their cattle, these songs serve several purposes, giving voice to everything we might feel about life: joy, fear, peace, confusion—any and every emotion. They also give voice to ideas about the nature of God: faithful, just, forgiving, holy—to name just a few of God's characteristics. Psalm 105 retells the story of God's covenant with Abraham, Isaac and Jacob (Joseph's father); and instructs people to praise God for His salvation, to trust Him because He fulfilled the covenant and to seek God and obey His commandments.

Have different volunteers read aloud verses of Psalm 105 as indicated below and then discuss each section, making sure that the points below are covered in each discussion.

- Verses 1-7: The song begins by instructing people to praise God, to sing about what He has done, to recall His wondrous works. It's like an invitation to sit around the kitchen table and say, "Hey, remember when God . . .?" God wants us to tell His stories.

- Verses 8-11: It's not only we who are called to remember. God remembers too! He remembers the promise He made to His people to be with them, to aid them, to bless them. God isn't an shapless blob; He has thought and memory, and He uses them! He remembers what He said, just as He asks us to remember those things as well.

- Verses 12-15: We are to remember the patriarchs—Abraham, Isaac and Jacob—and how God watched over them while they moved to a new land. (Though these stories aren't covered in this study, ask the group if they can identify the events being referred to in these verses.)

- Verses 16-22: We are to remember the life of Joseph and how he never lost faith in God, and God made him successful. Encourage volunteers to tell the specific events being called to mind in this passage.

OLD WEST CHARACTERS

WONG KIM ARK (BORN c. 1871)

The growth of the railroad industry in the Old West led many companies to hire workers from China, who were often given the dangerous blasting work. By the late 1800s, many Chinese immigrants had settled in San Francisco. One such individual, named Wong Kim Ark, visited China in 1894 and, on returning home, was denied readmittance because he was not deemed a citizen. He sued in court, and eventually his case was heard before the U.S. Supreme Court. In a landmark decision, the court ruled that a person born in the U.S. was a legal U.S. citizen, regardless of whether his or her parents were citizens.

Photo: National Archives and Records Administration. Public domain.

- Verses 23-25: Joseph's family moved to Egypt, and God made the family grow until the Israelites were so numerous that the Egyptians began to worry that they might rebel against their slavery.

- Verses 26-41: After God sent plagues to Egypt, He had Moses lead the Israelites out of Egypt. Invite volunteers to point out the references to the Exodus story that they know, and as needed, fill in any details, such as about the Israelites wandering in the desert (described in verses 39-41).

- Verses 42-45: God fulfilled His promise to give His Chosen People the Promised Land, and the people rejoiced. The first half of the last verse points out the goal of all that God had done: He wanted His people to obey His commandments in order to become holy like He is.

Point out to the group that we too are heirs to the covenant, because through Abraham, "all peoples on earth will be blessed" (Genesis 12:3). In Jesus, all of God's intentions were ultimately fulfilled, and He has blessed us by redeeming us.

Once everyone has a clear sense of what Psalm 105 calls them to remember, have the group members form seven small groups. Hand out paper and colored markers, and assign each group one of the seven sections of the song you just read and discussed. Instruct the group members to create "photos" of the events and ideas in their assigned section of the song. As group members finish drawings, insert the drawings in order in the photo album. Once the album is complete, have each group tell about their drawing(s).

Explain that remembering what God has done allows us to recall who God is and His intentions and will for His people. We can also recall that He has worked in the lives of His people to save them, and He works in our lives and intends that through Jesus, we will be saved too. Memories of Bible stories keep our hearts in tune with God and our minds focused on His truth.

DIG

Live for Him. For this activity, you'll need Bibles, a copy of "Remember This" (found on the next two pages) for each group member, and pens or pencils.

Hand out Bibles, copies of "Remember This," and pens or pencils. Point out to the group members that it's no accident that the stories of Joseph and Moses make up the bulk of Psalm 105. Their stories have far-reaching lessons

REMEMBER THIS

Through the lives of Joseph and Moses, we learn a lot about persevering and about how God intended and willed that His people be redeemed. Both men had to hang on to their faith in God through some very difficult times, but they both saw that through those times, God always intended good.

JOSEPH

See how well you remember the details of Joseph's life from Genesis 37; 39–41. (You can use your Bibles if you need to.) What two dreams did Joseph have that made his family angry?

_____

_____

_____

How did Joseph end up in Egypt?

_____

_____

_____

What was Joseph's first "job" in Egypt, and how good was he at it?

_____

_____

_____

Why did Joseph end up in prison, and how good was he at the job he had in prison?

_____

_____

_____

How did Joseph end up before Pharaoh, and what did he do for Pharaoh?

_____

_____

_____

What did Pharaoh do for Joseph?

_____

_____

_____

When we remember how Joseph kept his heart faithful to God despite betrayal, slavery and imprison-ment, we find encouragement to stay true as well. When we remember God's Word, we find strength to persevere through trials.

MOSES

Now let's see how well you recall the details of Moses' life from Exodus 2:1-10; 3–12. (If you need to use your Bibles, go ahead!) To what people group did Moses belong?

_____

_____

_____

How did Moses end up being raised in the Egyptian court?

_____

_____

_____

_____

How did Moses end up living as a shepherd in Midian?

_____

_____

_____

How did God reveal Himself to Moses, and what did God say His name was?

_____

_____

_____

How did the Israelites remain safe during the last plague, and how is that event celebrated today?

_____

_____

_____

_____

When we remember Moses, we see how God used a man who didn't feel qualified or capable to res-cue a whole nation of slaves. What gave Moses courage to endure through the difficulties? He remem-bered the words God had spoken and kept going back to what God had said. We can do the same.

that encourage us to remember what God intends and wills for us. Have group members form pairs to work together to answer the questions on the handout. After the handouts are complete, gather the group members together and invite volunteers to share their responses.

Once the group members have shared their ideas, have a volunteer read aloud James 1:12. Invite volunteers to tell how Joseph and Moses "stood the test." Remind the group that although Jesus was God, He became a man. Then invite other volunteers to tell how Jesus "stood the test." Point out that it cost Jesus His life to redeem us, but He did. This act of love should be the ultimate word of encouragement when we feel like giving up. It should also remind us that God's intentions and His will for us can never be stopped.

APPLY

Move *to* Him. For this activity, you'll need a copy of the chorus of "Jingle Bells" (or some other well-known song of your choosing) for every group member and pens or pencils. For after the session, you'll also need a copier (or a computer and printer) and a stapler.

Explain that songs are an important component of culture and serve several purposes. For cowboys in the Old West, singing songs during guard duty at night calmed the cattle, kept the cowboys awake, and let each other know where they were. Songs were also sung around the campfire and while on the trail for entertainment purposes. The songs covered a wide range of subjects, each touching somehow on something personal or something on the ranch or the trail, usually commemorating a significant event or place or person. It's a proven fact that we remember things better when they are put to music. It's why someone can recall thousands of song lyrics but not remember a good friend's birthday or last week's vocabulary words. So now's the time to make God's work in our lives something to remember!

Instruct the group to create the lyrics for a song that highlights a specific aspect of God's nature (such as His faithfulness, power or love) and put the words to the music of "Jingle Bells" (or some other well-known song of your choosing). Group members can also include in their lyrics how God has specifically worked in their lives. The bottom line is to create something memorable that can teach someone else something about God that would encourage him or her to believe in God and be redeemed. (If the group needs help getting started, suggest that one way to begin could be "Oh, faithful God, faithful God/Faithful to His word.")

After the group members have created their lyrics, have the group sit in a circle, as around a campfire, and invite a few volunteers to share their lyrics, either reading them or singing them. Finally, collect all the lyrics, type them up and make copies to create a songbook of memories for each group member.

End the session by praying for the group, thanking God for sending Jesus to fulfill God's will and intention to redeem them. Also thank God for the gift of music.

REFLECT

Be *with* Him. The following short devotions are for group members to reflect on and answer during the week. You can make copies of these pages and distribute them to your group members, or you can download and print the pages from **www.gospellight.com/uncommon/jh_Jesus_is_with_me.zip.**

1—REMEMBER THE BASICS

Read 2 Peter 1:12-15. Why is it important to remind yourself of things that you already know about God?

_____

_____

_____

_____

Just as cowboys practice again and again in order to be able to lasso a steer or a horse, what basics about faith in Jesus can you practice again and again?

_____

_____

_____

_____

What are a few ways you can remind yourself about how great God is?

_____

_____

_____

_____

Spend a minute thinking about the truth you know, and then ask God to help
you remember it throughout the day.

2—REMEMBER CONFESSION

Read Psalm 25:6-7. What does David want God to remember?

_____

_____

_____

What does David want God not to remember?

_____

_____

_____

Read Hebrews 8:12. What does God promise us?

_____

_____

_____

Take a minute and confess to the One who will forgive and forget those sins
that still weigh on you.

3—REMEMBER JESUS

Read 2 Timothy 2:8. What should we remember?

_____

_____

_____

_____

Read 1 Corinthians 15:3-4. What are the three main points we are to remember about Jesus?

_____

_____

_____

Take a minute to thank God for giving us His Word, the Bible. Ask God to help you remember to read it every day, because it is the basis for everything we are as God's children.

4—REMEMBER OTHERS

Read Matthew 28:19-20; Mark 16:15-16. What did Jesus tell His disciples to do?

_____

_____

_____

Why is this such an important thing to do (see Mark 16:16)?

_____

_____

_____

Take a minute and pray about who you can share the gospel with today. Then do it!

ULTIMATE ALLEGIANCE

THE BIG IDEA

We obey only God's commands, because we hear the voice of our loving Father, our caring Shepherd, in them.

SESSION AIMS

In this session, group members will (1) see how God wanted His people to listen and obey only Him, (2) realize that obedience to God's Word brings blessings into our lives, and (3) recognize that Jesus wants us to listen and obey only Him.

THE BIGGEST VERSES

"My sheep listen to my voice; I know them, and they follow me. I give them eternal life, and they shall never perish; no one can snatch them out of my hand" (John 10:27-28).

OTHER IMPORTANT VERSES

Deuteronomy 4–5; 1 Samuel 3; Psalms 23:1; 29; Isaiah 30:21; Romans 8:13-14; Hebrews 3:7-19

Most people hear the word "cowboy" and think of cattle drives in the Old West, but there were cowboys in other parts of the country as well. Cowboys in other parts of the country were similar to cowboys out West, differing mainly in the tools they used to herd cattle or bring cattle back to the herd. In the West, the herding was done mainly with ropes (think *lassos*); in places like Florida, however, the herding was done mainly with bullwhips and dogs.[1]

The intelligent canines used to help drive herds across long distances nimbly navigated in and out of the cows to keep them moving and together. And the dogs themselves were perfect for the job: quick, agile, confident, obedient and low-maintenance. In fact, a cattle dog was so responsive to a cowboy's commands that it could hear and obey cues accurately even amid the noise of the trail. The dog listened for the voice of its master, knew the voice well and followed it faithfully.

Likewise, God wants us to draw so close to Him in a loving, committed relationship that we hear His voice above the noise of the world and obey what He says with joyful diligence. To help us, He gave us His Word—a recorded revelation—as a way for us to "hear" Him without fail so that we can follow Him without fail.

STARTER

Depend *on* Him. You'll need a CD recording of famous people speaking and a CD player. (If it's possible to make your own recording, include on the CD the voice of your pastor, your own voice and the voices of a couple of well-known people in the news and/or who report the news.) Ahead of time, cue the CD to play the first voice.

Explain that recognizing someone by their voice usually gets easier the longer we know someone, because the longer we know someone, the more familiar we become with their voice and how they speak. Play the first voice (someone whose voice the group members are sure to know) and have group members tell to whom the voice belongs. Once the voice is identified, play the next voice and again have the group identify the speaker. Continue playing a few more voices, ending with the voice of someone with whom the group members are probably not familiar. Ideally, you will be able to help the group see that they are more likely to recognize the voice of someone they have heard speak a lot than someone they only hear talk from time to time.

Next, point out that when God gave His commandments to the Israelites, He meant for His Chosen People to hear His voice in His commands—the voice of a loving Father, a caring Shepherd. God wanted to make sure that His people were devoted only to Him and listened only to Him. The commandments of God were just a written expression of His love for them and a way to ensure that they live the best lives possible.

MESSAGE

Learn *from* **Him.** You'll need a whiteboard and erasable marker or a flip chart and marker, Bibles, one copy of "Hear My Voice" (found on the following two pages) for each group member, and pens or pencils.

Invite any volunteers to identify some of the Ten Commandments. As the volunteers identify the commandments, write them on the whiteboard or flip chart so that everyone can keep track of them. Once all the commandments have been listed, remind the group that these rules were given by God to His Chosen People in the context of relationship. God chose the Israelites, delivered them, guided them and provided for them. When it came time for Him to give them guidelines on how to live their lives, He Himself came down to Moses and spoke His words to him and the people. For Christians, relationship always precedes godly living, and we need to be connected to the Holy One before we can live holy lives. The rules that God gave were meant to enable His people to live the best lives possible.

By way of background, explain that "Deuteronomy" means "repetition of the law." The law was given the first time at Mount Sinai to the older generation of Israelites, the ones who had been delivered from Egypt. Those people had heard God's awesome, thunderous voice and had witnessed His mighty power. Unfortunately, they had not completely trusted God and, as a result, had wandered through the desert for 40 years and died there.

What Deuteronomy records is Moses' last words to the new generation of Israelites, those who would enter the Promised Land. (Don't forget to mention, though, that because Joshua and Caleb had believed God and had never doubted His promises, they were the only two of the older generation who were going to be allowed to enter the Promised Land.) Moses repeated for the new generation the Ten Commandments because he wanted them to realize that only by following God's commandments would they prosper in the land God was giving them. Obedience would be the key to their success.

Hand out copies of "Hear My Voice" and pens or pencils. Have group members work in pairs to complete the handout. When they are finished, gather everyone back together and review the group's responses.

Hear My Voice

Listen up! See if you can hear what God was saying to His people in these passages. Read Deuteronomy 4:1-8. What were the Israelites instructed to not do with God's commandments (see verse 2)?

_____
_____
_____
_____

What would the Israelites gain by following God's rules (see verses 1,4-6)?

_____
_____
_____

What would others say about the Israelites if they observed God's commands (see verse 6)?

_____
_____
_____

What two things would make Israel a great nation (see verses 7-8)?

_____
_____
_____
_____

Read Deuteronomy 4:9-14. What two things were the Israelites told to do with what they had seen and heard (see verses 9-10)?

_____
_____
_____

Read Deuteronomy 4:15-31. Why did God forbid the worship of idols (see verses 15-16,20,23-24)?

_____
_____

Read Deuteronomy 4:32-40. Why did God do all the things He did (see verses 35-36)?

_____

_____

_____

_____

Read Deuteronomy 5:1-21. Why was it important that the Israelites be reminded that God had made a covenant with them (see verses 1-3)?

_____

_____

_____

_____

Why did the Israelites need to hear the Ten Commandments?

_____

_____

_____

_____

_____

Read Deuteronomy 5:22-27. God did what two things with His commands to the people (see verse 22), and why were both things important?

_____

_____

_____

_____

_____

How did God's voice sound to the Israelites, and what did they think would happen to them (see verses 23-26)?

_____

_____

_____

_____

What did the Israelites promise to do about God's commandments (see verse 27)?

_____

_____

_____

Make sure you mention the points given below:

- Deuteronomy 4:1-8: Hearing is always connected with actions such as "follow," "observe" or "watch." So hearing involves *doing*, or obeying. Obedience keeps us safe (see verses 3-4) and makes us wise (see verse 6). Both God's presence and His laws are emphasized, because they are both gifts and are meant to be enjoyed together (see verses 7-8). This is sort of like a cattle dog hearing its master's voice and immediately acting to obey the command it's given.

- Deuteronomy 4:9-14: It's easy to let things slip when we don't purposefully keep them in front of us (see verse 9). One way to keep things fresh is by teaching someone else what we know (see verse 10). We *learn* reverence just as we *learn* obedience—both of which come from *hearing* and *doing* God's Word (see verse 10). The commandments were the foundation for living in the Promised Land; forgetting them would jeopardize the Israelites' success in the new land (see verses 13-14). In the case of most herding dogs, a young dog is trained not only by the cowboy who owns it but also by the older dog who has been doing the job for years. The young dog hears from the cowboy, learns from the older dog and then does what is commanded.

OLD WEST CHARACTERS

LAURA INGALLS WILDER (1867–1957)

Laura Ingalls Wilder was an American author who is best known for her Little House on the Prairie series of books. She was born in the "Big Woods" of Wisconsin and grew up on the prairies of what is now Independence, Kansas. She began teaching at the age of 16 to help support her family, but quit two years later when she married Almanzo Wilder, who was 10 years her senior. Inspired by her daughter, Rose, she began writing in 1911 and landed a position as a columnist for a local paper. She published *Little House in the Big Woods* in 1931, which lauched her career as a writer. She died in 1957 at the age of 90.

- Deuteronomy 4:15-31: God forbade the worship of other gods, because He is jealous of anything that takes His people away from Him (see verses 15-24). The Israelites are warned that if they ever forgot God and His commandments, they would be scattered among the nations of the world (see verses 25-27). A herding dog forgetting a command and doing something incorrectly—like barking at the wrong moment—could actually stampede a herd or lead to strays wandering off and getting lost.

- Deuteronomy 4:32-40: God initiated everything that happened. He spoke; He redeemed; He disciplined. "Discipline" in this context does not mean "punish" (verse 36). Rather, It means to train, to disciple. Sometimes that training may feel a little painful, especially when we are being corrected. However, God's discipline is not punitive; it is empowering. And all discipline is because of His great love (see verse 37). A well-trained dog becomes well trained by daily practicing the skills it knows. Repetition may not be a lot of fun, but repeated practice is necessary to maintain proper training and so that responses come quickly, almost automatically.

- Deuteronomy 5:1-21: Moses reminded the Israelites that God made a covenant with them and God "spoke to [them] face to face" (verse 4). Then Moses repeated the Ten Commandments so that the Israelites would remember them and obey them. Remind the group that the generation that Moses was addressing was a new generation; their parents, who had heard God first speak the Ten Commandments, had died in the desert, so a repetition of the commandments was necessary so that there would be no misunderstanding of God's requirements.

- Deuteronomy 5:22-27: This is a continuation of the conversation that started in chapter 4, and it refers again to the Mount Sinai experience. The commands of God were *spoken* first so the people would know they came from God (see verse 22). Then God *wrote* them down and gave them to Moses (see verse 22). God wanted to be sure that the Israelites had the right rules and would know how He wanted them to live. Have the group look for every time "hear" or "listen" is used in this passage: "when you heard" (verse 23), "we have heard" (verse 24), "if we hear" (verse 25), "heard the voice" (verse 26), "go near and listen" (verse 27), "we will listen" (verse 27).

Conclude by stating that it's clear that the event on Mount Sinai involved God's Word being sounded out and God's people hearing it. God's voice was not an unknown voice but a known one—the voice of the One who had rescued them from slavery and now was teaching them how to live. They needed to hear Him speak so that they would know whom to follow. For cowboys, a well-trained dog knows the voice of the cowboy who trained it and feeds it. This close relationship helps keep the dog from being distracted by the words of others—so much so that a command from someone else will not be obeyed; only the recognized voice of its owner will be followed.

DIG

Live *for* Him. For this activity, you'll need a Bible, the same number of balloons as you have group members—all but one of the balloons should be the same color—and a blindfold. Ahead of time, blow up and tie off the balloons.

Explain that listening for God's voice takes practice, and we have to listen carefully so that we aren't led astray or distracted from what God says to us. Have the group sit around in a circle, and place all of the balloons in the circle. Invite one volunteer to be the Shepherd and one volunteer to be the Sheep. Explain that the Shepherd is to speak in a normal voice to give the Sheep, who is to remain silent, instructions for finding the balloon that is a different color. The rest of the group tries to distract the Sheep by whispering about other things. Blindfold the Sheep and have him or her stand in the middle of the circle. Mix up the balloons, and invite the Shepherd to begin giving instructions while the rest of the group whispers.

Once the Sheep picks up the correct balloon, briefly discuss how the relationship between a shepherd and his or her sheep is used to describe the relationship between Jesus and His people—believers, or us. Read aloud John 10:27-28. Jesus knows His people—His sheep, us—and we know Him. His voice is familiar to us, we trust Him to protect us, and He wants us to follow His every instruction so that we will always be safe, even eternally.

Then read aloud John 10:2-5,14. Invite volunteers to tell what "strangers" or sorts of things "whisper" to distract us from hearing God's voice (for example, hobbies, sports, friends, clothes, the Internet, music). Invite other volunteers to tell how we can show that we are members of Jesus' flock (for example, pray, study the Bible, worship with other Christians, hang out with other Christians, or be kind to others). Suggest that the group members choose one of the ways to concentrate on doing this week.

APPLY

Move *to* Him. For this activity, you need a Bible, a slab of self-hardening clay (available at craft and hobby stores) for each member, and a round toothpick.

Read aloud Hebrews 8:8-12. Explain that the law that God gave is no longer external—written on a stone tablets. Instead, when we received Jesus, God wrote His law on our hearts. In other words, He changed us on the inside so that we could truly know Him and hear His voice.

Hand out a small lump of clay and a toothpick to each group member. Have each group member shape the clay into a heart and write on it something from today's Bible story or from John 10:27-28 ("God's commands," "Hearing means obeying," "I know Jesus' voice," "Jesus is my Shepherd").

Invite volunteers to share what they wrote and why. Remind the group that obedience to God's Word brings blessings into their lives, and spend a few minutes in prayer, having the group commit to lives of hearing and obeying God. Suggest to the group that they take their heart tablets home, let them dry, paint them and use them as small paperweights to remind them to listen to God's voice.

End the session by praying for the group, asking God to help them listen only to His voice and be devoted only to Him.

REFLECT

Be *with* Him. The following short devotions are for group members to reflect on and answer during the week. You can make copies of these pages and distribute them to your group members, or you can download and print the pages from **www.gospellight.com/uncommon/jh_Jesus_is_with_me.zip.**

1—LISTEN TO GOD SPEAK

Read the following Old Testament verses and tell which ways God spoke to His people:

Genesis 15:1: _____

Genesis 28:10-15: _____

Exodus 31:18: _____

2 Kings 17:13: _____

Read Hebrews 1:1-2. What was God's final revelation of how He spoke to His people?

_____

_____

_____

_____

_____

How can you listen to Jesus? One way is to read about His life. Take a minute and commit to read a chapter a day in one of the Gospels (the books of Matthew, Mark, Luke or John). As you read, jot down what you see in Jesus and what His actions and words teach you.

2—HAVE FAITH

Read Hebrews 4:1-7. When the Israelites first arrived at Canaan, why weren't they able to enter the Promised Land? What had they lacked (see verse 2)?

_____

_____

_____

_____

What should we be careful about, now that we've been invited to hear Jesus' voice today (see verse 7)?

_____

_____

_____

_____

Read James 2:17. How does a person show that he or she has faith?

_____

_____

_____

_____

Take a minute to ask God to help you not only read God's Word and hear it preached but to also believe what God has to say and to help you act on it.

3—ACT IN FAITH

When you look in the mirror, you are usually fixing something: brushing messy hair, scrubbing dirt off your face, washing cookie crumbs out of your teeth. The mirror shows us what we look like and enables us to see well enough to change what needs to be changed. The Word of God is similar. When we read it or hear it, we learn what God wants us to be like, and then we can take steps to get there. Read James 1:19-25. What should we be quick to do, and what should we accept (see verses 19,21)?

_____

_____

_____

_____

_____

What happens when we hear the Word of God and don't do it, and what happens when we hear the Word of God and do it (see verses 23-25)?

_____

_____

_____

_____

_____

How can you show faith in action today?

_____

_____

_____

_____

Take a minute to take a good look at yourself in terms of God's Word. Then pray that God will help you to do what it says.

4—BUILD ON SOLID GROUND

Read Luke 6:46-49 (Matthew 7:24-27 covers the same ground, no pun intended). When a crisis or a problem or some other sort of trouble has to be faced by a person who hasn't built his or her life on obeying and trusting Jesus, what happens to that person (see verse 49)?

_____

_____

_____

_____

When a crisis or a problem or some other sort of trouble has to be faced by a person who *has* built his or her life on obeying and trusting Jesus, what happens to that person (see verses 47-48)?

_____

_____

_____

_____

Take a few minutes to consider how much of your life—your attitudes, your values, your choices—is based on obedience to God's Word and how much is based on your own ideas. What areas of your life are founded on solid ground, and what areas need to be strengthened?

_____

_____

_____

_____

Spend a few minutes in prayer, asking for God's help to make sure the foundation of your life is God's Word. Also ask God to help you obey and trust that what He says is good. Then act on it!

ULTIMATE LEGACY

THE BIG IDEA
God wants every generation to learn to love and obey Him and to teach the next generation to love and obey Him.

SESSION AIMS
In this session, group members will (1) see how God commanded parents to obey Him so they could teach their children His truth, (2) realize each generation is meant to pass on to the next generation what they learn about loving and obeying God, and (3) see that Jesus left us a legacy of faith to model.

THE BIGGEST VERSES
"Hear, O Israel: The LORD our God, the LORD is one. Love the LORD your God with all your heart and with all your soul and with all your strength. These commandments that I give to you today are to be upon your hearts. Impress them upon your children" (Deuteronomy 6:4-7).

OTHER IMPORTANT VERSES
Deuteronomy 6; Psalms 22:30-31; 78:1-7; Matthew 12:50; Acts 2:38-39; 16:1; Philippians 4:9

It's true that experience is often the best teacher. What we have struggled to learn can change the life of someone who has yet to walk that path—if we are willing to pass our wisdom along.

The cowboys and settlers of the Old West relied on such advice and found that accepting the time-tested wisdom of those who had "been there, done that" made life significantly easier and better. When someone found a natural spring hidden among the mountains or a shortcut that really did save days of travel or a wild herb that could stave off infection until a doctor could be found, that knowledge was shared in hopes of helping the other cowboys and settlers survive. The information was then passed on to the less-experienced people so that they too would reap its benefits.

When God gave His rules to the Israelites, He commanded them not only to live by the rules themselves but also to pass them along to future generations. What they learned about obeying God was meant to benefit their children and their grandchildren and every future generation. We too are called by God to hand down God's commandments to the next generation so that they can learn to obey God and grow in His grace just as we have (we *have,* right!). God's commandments must be passed along, and Jesus will help every generation obey Him!

STARTER

Depend *on* **Him.** For this activity, you'll need a dozen tennis balls, and some snacks for prizes. (Ahead of time, check to make sure that no one is allergic to the food you provide.)

Welcome group members, have them take off their shoes and invite them to sit shoulder to shoulder in two equal lines, legs out straight. Place half the tennis balls in a pile at one end of each line. Explain that at your signal, each team is to pass its tennis balls from one end of the line to the other, but only feet may be used to pass the balls. The balls cannot touch the floor at any time, except at the beginning and end of each line. Signal the teams to start.

After a certain amount of time has passed, signal the end of the game and count how many balls each team passed successfully. Reward the winning team with a snack—and then shell out the snack to the other team as well.

At the end of play, note for the group that each person had to both *receive* and *pass along* a tennis ball in order to keep things moving. If one person either didn't receive or couldn't pass it along, the whole process came to a halt. Explain that today's session focuses on the way God expects His commands to be handled by His people: Not only are we to receive and obey them, but we also are to pass them along to the next generation so others can experience God's blessings and goodness.

MESSAGE

Learn *from* **Him.** You'll need Bibles, paper, pens or pencils, and a copy of "Commandments for Life" (found on the next two pages) for each group member.

Pass out paper and pens or pencils. Have the group members form groups of four or five and tell them they are going to be starting a new country in which to live. Direct them to brainstorm the rules—if any—that will govern the people of their land. Give groups five to seven minutes to note down their ideas and then have each group share their ideas. Invite volunteers to tell what rules would be most helpful and why; what it would be like to live without any rules; why rules are important; and what is the best way to pass along rules.

Briefly go over why passing information, such as rules, along to others is important. Note that in the Old West, passing along information about such things as mountain passes that would save trouble, time or wear and tear on people, animals and wagons; beneficial herbs that could save a life while a doctor's help was sought; and such things as waterholes was extremely important for the survival of the cowboys and settlers in the region. The need to pass on God's commandments to the next generation is even more important because living by God's commandments allows us to receive God's blessings.

Then point out to the group that the words God gave His people were meant to guide them to be successful in their new lives in the Promised Land. When we realize that God's commandments are meant not to stifle us but to guide us, we can trust that what He requires of us is for our good—and for the good of the future generations.

Give each group member a Bible, a copy of "Commandments for Life" and a pen or pencil. Have everyone work independently to complete the handout. Then review the group's responses, highlighting the points made below:

- Deuteronomy 6:1-3: God's "commands, decrees and laws" were meant for all generations: for "you, your children and their children" (verse 2). The results of obeying all of God's commands would be the following: "enjoy long life," "it may go well with you," and "you may increase greatly" (verses 2-3). These ideas indicate that the rules are for our benefit and are meant for each generation to learn and follow.

COMMANDMENTS FOR LIFE

Read Deuteronomy 6:1-3. For whom were the commands intended?

_____
_____
_____
_____

What would be the results of obeying all of God's commands?

_____
_____
_____
_____

What does this tell us about the purpose of God's Word?

_____
_____
_____
_____

Read Deuteronomy 6:4-9. List the different ways, times and places that God's laws are to permeate our lives.

Three ways:

_____
_____
_____

Four times:

_____
_____
_____

Four places:

_____
_____
_____

What does this tell us about how God's rules are to affect our day-to-day living?

_____

_____

_____

_____

_____

Read Deuteronomy 6:10-19. Why is it so important that we remember all that God has done?

_____

_____

_____

_____

_____

Read Deuteronomy 6:20-25. Why did the Israelite parents begin their explanation about obeying God's commandments with the story of the Exodus from Egypt?

_____

_____

_____

_____

How is God's love reflected in His commandments?

_____

_____

_____

_____

Why would God tell parents to pass along His rules? Why not just reveal Himself to each generation?

_____

_____

_____

_____

In what way(s) does obeying God's commands lead us to "always prosper and be kept alive" (verse 24)?

_____

_____

_____

_____

_____

- Deuteronomy 6:4-9: God's commandments were meant to apply to all parts our lives. Mentioned in the passage are three different ways (heart, soul and strength—verse 5); at four different times (when at home, while walking, while lying down and while getting up—verse 7); and in four different places (hands, foreheads, doorframes and gates—verse 8). God's commandments are not for special occasions. They are to penetrate our whole being, from the attitudes of our hearts to places we go to things we do. They are meant to govern our entire existence.

- Deuteronomy 6:10-19: God's commandments were meant to never be forgotten, because keeping them would help prevent God's people from following idols and from relying on their own strength, which wasn't what got them where they were now—*God* had rescued them from slavery.

- Deuteronomy 6:20-25: God's commandments were meant to be passed along to the next generation. Parents were to begin their discussion about obeying God's commandments with the story of the Exodus in order to set the commandments in the proper context: God's love. God gave the Israelites His laws and decrees because of His love for them and His desire to see them live free, prosperous, holy lives.

OLD WEST CHARACTERS

FREDERIC REMINGTON (1861–1909)

Frederic Remington was a painter and sculptor who specialized in creating depictions from the Old West. He first became interested in drawing such scenes at the age of 19 when he took a camping trip to Montana. In 1887, he was asked to do 83 illustrations for a book by Theodore Roosevelt, which sparked a long-term friendship. He was frequently sent on assignment to cover U.S. troop actions in the Old West, where he would paint portraits of Army officers. By the time of his death, his fame had grown to such an extent that other Western painters were known as being in the "School of Remington."

Conclude by stating that God knows best how we should live our lives, and His commandments will guide us toward the goal He has for us. We have to remember that it is because of His love for us that He gave us His commandments, and His commandments lead to blessing (verses 24-25).

DIG

Live *for* Him. For this activity, you'll need Bibles, a whiteboard and erasable marker or a flip chart and marker, old magazines, scissors, glue, paper, markers, a three-hole punch and a large binder.

Explain to the group that Jesus was an example of what a legacy of faith looks like. Jesus, who learned obedience from His Father, told us that to show that we love Him, we also need to obey the Father. We need to follow Jesus' example of humbling Himself and doing the Father's will. By learning what Jesus had to say to us, by doing what He told us to do and by looking at the legacy He left for us, we too can strive to be perfect like Him and to pass on a legacy of faith. Jesus even told us to pass on what we have learned. Invite a volunteer to read aloud Matthew 5:14-16. Comment that we are to live out our faith so that others can in turn be attracted to faith in Jesus.

Hand out Bibles. Point out that one good way to remember our legacy from the past is by looking at photos, and although we do not have any photos of Jesus, we do have word pictures of Jesus in the New Testament. Brainstorm a list of images of Jesus in the New Testament, and as images are mentioned, list them and the reference on the whiteboard or flip chart. If the group has trouble thinking of images, list some of the following: Jesus said He was "the bread of life" (John 6:35); other images include "living water" (John 4:10); "the light of the world" (John 8:12); "the gate" (John 10:9); "the good shepherd" (John 8:12); "the resurrection," which could be symbolized by a cross (John 11:25); "the way and the truth and the life" (John 14:6); "the true vine" (John 15:1); "God is love" (1 John 4:8).

When you have completed this step, spread out the magazines, scissors and glue, and then hand everyone a sheet of paper and a marker. Instruct the group members that they are to use magazine pictures to create an image of Jesus for the binder. They can write some words or phrases beneath the image to describe it (for example, "Jesus is our Shepherd," or "Jesus died on a cross for our sins," or "God is love"). When everyone has completed their image, add the "photos" to the album and share the album with the group to review Jesus' legacy of faith to us.

APPLY

Move *to* Him. For this activity, you'll need Bibles, images of Jewish phylacteries from the Internet, tape; and for each group member a ½" x 3' strip of leather (or heavy fabric) and a permanent marker.

Read aloud Deuteronomy 6:8, which instructs the people to "tie [God's commandments] as symbols on your hands and bind them on your foreheads." Explain that some Jewish men today literally strap to their foreheads and left arms small black boxes containing particular Bible verses as reminders to love God with their minds and with their strength. These boxes and straps are symbols of the kind of intentional devotion and obedience God asked of them. When exactly the phylacteries are worn varies with the beliefs of the wearer. Show the images of the phylacteries, and then tape the images to a wall where the group can see them.

Give each group member a Bible, a strip of leather and a marker. Instruct each group member to write Deuteronomy 6:5 on the strap. Then have them tie the strap around their left arms, mimicking what they see in the images. Since this is just a symbol, it doesn't need to be done perfectly. The idea is to experience a little of what some Jewish men do to remind themselves that they are to recognize only one God and obey and love Him with all their hearts, souls and strength—that they are committed to obeying God's commandments.

End the session by praying for the group, thanking God for His love and His commandments, and asking Him to help the group pass on to others their love of and obedience to God.

REFLECT

Be *with* Him. The following short devotions are for group members to reflect on and answer during the week. You can make copies of these pages and distribute them to your group members, or you can download and print the pages from **www.gospellight.com/uncommon/jh_Jesus_is_with_me.zip**.

1—A LEGACY FROM THE OLD TESTAMENT

If you follow Jesus, you have been adopted into a family with a long line of faithful—but not perfect!—believers. Read Hebrews 11. What is faith (see verse 1)?

_____

_____

_____

Why are people of faith "aliens and strangers on earth" (see verses 13-16)?

_____

_____

_____

_____

Read Hebrews 12:1. The "great cloud of witnesses" represents the people from Hebrews 11. In what ways do people of faith cheer others on toward obedience?

_____

_____

_____

_____

_____

Take a minute to thank God for all of the stories of people of faith in the Old Testament, people who left us a legacy that encourages us to obey God and pass that legacy on to others.

2—A LEGACY FROM FAMILY

Read 2 Timothy 1:3-6. Paul's love of God follows whose example (see verse 3)?

_____

_____

_____

_____

Who was Lois, and who was Eunice (see verse 5)?

_____

_____

_____

_____

What did they pass along to Timothy, and what did Paul do to help?

_____

_____

_____

_____

Take a minute to consider who in your family (either your actual family or your church family) encourages you and helps you grow your faith. Now write something—a letter, an email, a text—to one of the people who has helped you, telling that person how he or she has been an inspiration and/or an encourager to you.

3—A LEGACY FROM FRIENDS

Sometimes God uses people other than family members to help us learn to obey God's commands. Read 1 Corinthians 4:14-17. What kind of relationship did the apostle Paul, the writer of this letter, have with the church members at Corinth (see verse 14)?

_____

_____

_____

_____

What kind of relationship did the apostle Paul have with Timothy (see verse 17)?

_____

_____

_____

 What about how Paul lived his life do you think he wanted other believers to "imitate" (verse 16)?

_____

_____

_____

_____

Take a minute to consider who in your life serves as an example of right Christian living—someone who models for you living out God's Word and His commands (maybe not perfectly, but does a good job of trying). Now write down something—a letter, an email, a text—to that model, telling that person how he or she has helped to grow your faith.

4—A LEGACY FROM ME

Your life of obedience benefits more than just yourself. When you obey God, you pave the way for others to do so as well. Read 1 Peter 3:15. What should you always be prepared to do?

_____

_____

_____

_____

_____

Read 1 Peter 3:1. How may an unbeliever be attracted to belief, even if you don't talk to him or her?

_____

_____

_____

_____

_____

Take a minute to think about the younger children in your life (siblings, neighbors, friends). They are watching how you live and learning what obeying God means. (Okay, you and I and God know that you're not perfect, but part of learning to obey God means learning to repent and move forward!) Now—yes, you guessed it—write something (a letter, an email, a text) or draw a picture to give to the child to encourage him or her to love and obey God. Pass along what you have learned about following Jesus.

ULTIMATE SUSTENANCE

THE BIG IDEA

Our sole source of provision—for spirit and body—is God.

SESSION AIMS

In this session, group members will (1) see how God allowed the Israelites to experience hardships in order to teach them to depend on His ability to provide, (2) realize that in every circumstance we can depend on God to provide what we need, and (3) see that Jesus wants us to rely only on Him.

THE BIGGEST VERSE

"He humbled you, causing you to hunger and then feeding you with manna, which neither you nor your fathers had known, to teach you that man does not live on bread alone but on every word that comes from the mouth of the LORD" (Deuteronomy 8:3).

OTHER IMPORTANT VERSES

Deuteronomy 8; Joshua 23:14; Psalm 37:16-17; Micah 6:8; 2 Corinthians 9:8; Galatians 3:10-14; Hebrews 2:10-11; 1 Peter 4:12-13

On cattle drives, while the boss was technically the man who owned the cattle, the cowboys knew the man who had the most power was the cook. The chuck wagon was the equivalent of a general store, and the cook was often not only the clerk of the store but also the group's doctor, surgeon, dentist and tailor. The cowboys knew to stay in the cook's good favor, because he was the one who controlled the source of their sustenance. In addition, if the cook was on their side, they had a better chance of getting their bedding or clothing patched, their buttons re-sewed, their cuts doctored (with a healthy dose of kerosene oil), and their hair cut.[1]

For the Israelites in the wilderness, God was their source of provision. As we discussed in session 4, when the people grumbled against Moses and Aaron, whining that back in Egypt they had "pots of meat" and "all the food" they wanted (Exodus 16:3), God sent them quail and manna. When they needed water, He purified it for them (see Exodus 15:22-27) or provided it from a rock (see Exodus 17:1-7). God led them through situations in which they had to depend completely and solely on Him. He was not only the source of their physical sustenance, but also the source of their very lives. He was their deliverer, their strength and their hope. Today, God will likewise bring us through situations in which we will have to depend solely upon Him. As with the Israelites, He wants us to acknowledge that all we have depends on Him.

STARTER

Depend *on* Him. For this activity, you'll need butcher paper (or a plastic tablecloth), cookie cutters and other tools for shaping dough, play dough (available at craft stores, or check the Internet for a recipe for homemade play dough), large paper plates, a small plastic trophy and candy (or some other snack food). Ahead of time, cover a table with butcher paper/tablecloth and arrange for a couple of adults to be artwork judges. (Also ahead of time, check to make sure that no one is allergic to the food you provide.)

Welcome the group and explain that today they'll be participating in an art show in order to win the coveted Michelangelo Trophy. Place the cookie cutters and other tools in a central area, and give each group member a lump of play dough and a large paper plate on which to work. Give the group five to seven minutes to create something spectacular with their dough and to stage it on the butcher-paper-covered display table. Ask each group member to explain his or her art piece to the judges. After everyone's shared, have the judges select a winner. Award the trophy, and then give out the snack to all the participants.

As group members eat the snack, remind them that the dough had to be pressed, pulled, cut and smoothed into the desired shape—the result didn't happen on its own. Just like the artwork had to be shaped, so too our lives are in a constant process of being shaped by God. God is constantly allowing us to see His ability to provide, teaching us to trust Him and depend on Him in ever-increasing ways, and conforming us more and more into the image of Jesus.

MESSAGE

Learn *from* Him. For this activity, you'll need Bibles.

Explain to the group that throughout this study, we have seen how difficult life was for those who made the decision to strike out and go into the Old West. There were often dangers around every corner, and people on the frontier had to rely on each other and their faith in God to get through the tough times. In the same way, the people in the Bible—such as Joseph and Moses—had to endure tough situations that taught them to trust God and depend only on Him. God used these experiences to shape them into people who would have a huge impact on the course of history.

Invite volunteers to tell what experiences helped shape Moses and Joseph. Then point out that the lives of Moses and Joseph teach us that our problems and challenges are not just painful experiences to be endured—that our trials and difficulties have no real value. They are the means of our learning to trust and depend on God and a means by which of each of us is shaped into the image of Jesus—with a result of eternal consequence! The right response in times of testing is obedience, because obedience is an act of faith, and faith is what pleases God and has an eternal reward.

Pass out Bibles and have the group turn to Deuteronomy 8. Have different volunteers read aloud verses from the chapter and then discuss each passage, being sure to cover the points below:

- Deuteronomy 8:1: If the people obeyed God's commands, He promised they would "live and increase and may enter and possess the land." The commands God gave to His people were for their benefit— an idea that is presented consistently throughout the Scriptures. In the same way, obedience to God's commands is to our benefit.

- Deuteronomy 8:2: God placed the Israelites in difficult situations "to humble . . . and to test" them. God wanted the Israelites to realize that they should and could depend only on Him to provide for them. To see whether or not they had learned this lesson, He humbled them, showing them that it was only through God that they would survive; they could not survive through only their own efforts. In times of testing (both of the Israelites and of us), God is with those who believe in Him. God does not "push us out of the nest" and hope we make it. He carefully guides our lives so that what we experience helps us become like Him. How? Testing humbles us and shows us our deep need for Jesus. Testing reveals what is in our hearts—both good and bad—and gives us the opportunity to change.

- Deuteronomy 8:3: Moses pointed out to the Israelites that the trial of not having enough to eat provided them with the chance to trust in God—to trust that He *would* provide for their needs even when it seemed impossible.

- Deuteronomy 8:4: In the midst of the hardships the Israelites experienced, they received unexpected blessings; God still showed them His kindness in tangible ways: He blessed them with clothes that didn't wear out—for 40 years! And it seems that they never noticed what God was doing for them. Evidently, they had taken these things for granted. We need to look for the ways that God shows us small kind-

OLD WEST CHARACTERS

GEORGE CUSTER (1839–1876)

George Armstrong Custer was a U.S. Army officer and cavalry commander who gained noteriety during the American Civil War (1861–1865). In 1873, Custer was selected to lead a cavalry unit against the Lakota and other Native American tribes, who were angry at the U.S. government for continually breaking treaty agreements. On June 28, 1876, Custer led a force of 700 men at the Battle of the Little Bighorn against the chiefs Sitting Bull, Crazy Horse, Gall and Lame White Man. Custer committed a number of tactical errors that led to the U.S. Army's defeat, with 268 soldiers killed. Among the dead were Custer and two of his brothers.

Photo: Unknown (c 1860–1865), Library of Congress. Public domain.

nesses—in the midst of good times and in the midst of difficulties—because they remind us to trust Him at *all* times.

- Deuteronomy 8:5: The testing of the Israelites in the desert *was* part of God's plan. That testing was meant to teach the Israelites to depend on God and to trust in Him fully. Because God loved the Israelites, He wanted them to grow into people of strong faith, so He disciplined them. Explain that discipline does not necessarily mean punishment. God's discipline is meant to train us, to correct us and to mold us to become more and more "holy." In other words, it is to make us become more and more like His Son, Jesus.

- Deuteronomy 8:6-9: The land the Israelites were going to possess was bountiful in many ways. Make sure the group notes that it was God who "is bringing" them into the land. The Promised Land was to be theirs because it was God's will that it be theirs. It was the Lord God who was providing it to them.

- Deuteronomy 8:10-14: It was important that the Israelites not forget God after they had eaten their fill, after they had had their needs satisfied. Moses wanted the Israelites to constantly remember God's goodness—as we should as well.

- Deuteronomy 8:15-18: The younger generation of Israelites needed to remember their past so that they would remember how God had always provided for them, just as He was providing for them now by giving them the Promised Land. Nothing the Israelites had done in the desert had sustained them; what they had came only from God. And it would be the same in the Promised Land.

- Deuteronomy 8:19-20: Obedience to the laws and commands of God would enable the Israelites to live and prosper. Disobedience would lead to destruction.

Drive home the idea that obeying God's commands leads to blessings from God, and disobedience leads to separation from God and destruction. It is God who provides us with all that we have, and if we forget God, He will remove His blessings from us. God is the ultimate source of all that we need.

DIG

Live *for* Him. For this activity, you'll need a copy of "Sustenance? What Sustenance?" (found on the next page) for each group member and yourself, and pens or pencils. Ahead of time, complete a copy of the word search so that you'll know where in the puzzle all of the words are located.

Briefly go over the fact that the "sustenance" God provides is abundant and meets both our physical and spiritual needs. Invite a few group members to tell some of the physical things with which God provides us (such as air, water, sunlight, plants, family, shelter or the Bible). Then invite a few group members to tell some of the spiritual things with which God provides us (such as the Holy Spirit, blessings, truth, redemption, forgiveness and His promises).

Pass out copies of "Sustenance? What Sustenance?" and pens or pencils. Invite the group to find as many of the words as they can in whatever time limit you set. At the end of the time limit, go over the word list, identifying whether the word meets a physical need or a spiritual need (and have a volunteer identify where the word is in the puzzle).

End the activity by emphasizing the fact that God loves us and that He is our ultimate source for all that we have and all that we need. God is also the source of anything we create because it is from God that we have brains, curiosity and imagination.

APPLY

Move *to* Him. For this activity, you will need Bibles. Pass out Bibles and have a volunteer read aloud Deuteronomy 8:3. Then invite different volunteers to read aloud the following passages from John 6. As each is read, discuss the questions indicated for each passage:

- Verses 31-33: Who is the source of all bread? (*God.*) What two breads are being referred to here? (*Manna and Jesus.*)

- Verse 35: What does human bread provide for a person's body? (*It satisfies hunger and keeps us healthy.*) In what ways is Jesus like spiritual bread? (*He gives us what we need to live both today and for all eternity.*)

- Verses 47-51: In what ways is Jesus better than manna? (*The Israelites had to collect manna every day and eat it right away; it sustained the people for a time but did not last. Jesus satisfies us completely and provides us with eternal life.*)

—— SUSTENANCE? ——
WHAT SUSTENANCE?

God is the ultimate source of our sustenance for this life and the next, and just some of the things with which He provides us can be found in this word search puzzle. Look at the word list below the letter grid, and find as many of the words in the letter grid as you can. (Words may be found horizontally, vertically, and diagonally, backward and forward. Some words may even overlap.)

U	S	G	N	I	S	S	E	L	B	K	P	C	S	R	S	O	F	G	L
Z	N	U	Y	A	P	H	P	Y	D	E	D	O	S	E	D	X	N	R	D
D	Z	D	F	T	C	A	T	I	R	F	V	M	E	D	N	L	I	A	C
G	I	E	E	R	I	I	T	S	R	S	F	M	N	E	E	I	A	C	R
E	T	S	U	R	N	S	E	I	S	I	S	A	L	M	I	V	R	E	C
Y	G	H	C	R	S	V	O	E	E	U	T	N	U	P	R	I	B	U	D
I	C	A	E	I	E	T	N	I	N	N	H	D	F	T	F	N	O	A	S
G	E	T	R	R	P	E	A	L	R	I	C	M	K	I	G	G	E	U	P
I	E	L	A	U	V	L	I	N	U	U	L	E	N	O	S	R	S	N	R
P	R	N	B	I	O	G	I	R	D	O	C	N	A	N	B	T	N	Z	O
Y	C	J	G	I	H	C	T	N	V	I	H	T	H	L	E	W	O	R	M
E	V	R	O	T	B	D	T	E	E	X	N	S	T	N	O	P	I	E	I
N	O	I	T	C	E	R	R	U	S	E	R	G	A	I	P	N	T	W	S
F	X	Y	C	O	R	R	E	C	T	I	O	N	F	O	O	D	A	O	E
G	U	I	D	A	N	C	E	D	S	D	C	F	A	I	T	H	V	P	S
H	A	G	N	I	N	I	A	R	T	E	F	A	M	I	L	Y	L	W	H
M	O	D	S	I	W	E	C	A	E	P	U	L	D	P	Q	M	A	N	O
K	V	L	N	E	N	C	O	U	R	A	G	E	M	E	N	T	S	X	P
A	V	C	Y	N	J	G	P	Y	L	N	T	Z	C	E	E	Y	E	N	F
F	G	D	J	U	K	I	U	X	H	E	B	V	H	R	F	D	G	G	S

Bible	curiosity	friends	power	sunlight
blessings	discipline	grace	promises	sustenance
brain	encouragement	guidance	redemption	thankfulness
bread	eternity	hope	resurrection	training
church	faith	love	safety	truth
commandments	family	patience	salvation	understanding
correction	food	peace	Son	water
courage	forgiveness	perseverance	Spirit (Holy)	wisdom

- Verses 53-58: Jesus was not suggesting we become cannibals, so what did He mean when He said these words? (*Both bread and blood help sustain life; and in this verse, eating the flesh and blood of Jesus refers to believing the fact that Jesus sacrificed His flesh and blood for the forgiveness of our sins. When we believe in Jesus—what He did with His flesh and blood—we acknowledge that He is the source of life. Like human bread, though, we must "partake" of Jesus daily in order to be sustained for life.*)

- Verses 68-69: What did Peter acknowledge about Jesus? (*Jesus is the only source of eternal life.*) Where can we learn "the words of eternal life"? (*In the Bible.*) How can we "partake" of Jesus daily? (*Read the Bible every day, study the Bible, pray every day, and so forth.*)

Finally, invite a volunteer to read aloud Hebrews 13:8. Explain that Jesus, the One who has "the words of eternal life," never changes. He is a constant in a world that is always changing. He is always with us, providing us with what we need when we need it. We can rely on Him in every situation—good and bad. He will provide our sustenance, even for eternal life.

End the session by praying for the group, thanking God for sending Jesus, for loving them and never changing, and for being there for them to depend on as they live each day in faith.

REFLECT

Be *with* **Him.** The following short devotions are for group members to reflect on and answer during the week. You can make copies of these pages and distribute them to your group members, or you can download and print the pages from **www.gospellight.com/uncommon/jh_Jesus_is_with_me.zip**.

1—REST IN GOD'S HANDS

Read Psalm 138:7-8 and Isaiah 64:8. According to these verses, what are we, and what is God?

_____

_____

_____

_____

_____

Although we have our own thoughts about what we want to do with our lives, who should also always be part of our planning, and why?

_____

_____

_____

_____

Sometimes in our lives, we can feel the pressure of God's hands, holding us in a difficult place. When we trust God—when we rest in His hands—He brings us into balance and we can have peace regardless of our situation. Are you completely trusting in God, or are you still struggling to to take the control? How can you let go and trust God more completely?

_____

_____

_____

_____

Take a minute to thank God for His love and for His assurance that He will fulfill His good purposes and plans for you. Ask for His help to depend only on Him and to rest in His hands.

2—BE WILLING AND RECEPTIVE

Read Jeremiah 18:4-10. What did the potter do to the clay as Jeremiah watched, and why did the potter do this (see verse 4)?

_____

_____

_____

What did God say His people were like, and what would He do if people repented of wrongdoing (see verses 7-8)? What would He do if people continued to do wrong things (see verses 9-10)?

_____

_____

_____

Read James 1:2-4. Why must we depend only on God and be willing to be under God's control?

_____

_____

_____

_____

_____

Spend a minute in prayer to ask God to help you give everything over to Him in full obedience so that He can continue to work His perfect plan in your life.

3—HUMBLE YOURSELF

What does the word "humble" mean? (You might need a dictionary to find out!)

_____

_____

_____

_____

_____

Read Proverbs 3:34 and 1 Peter 5:6. What does God give to us when we humble ourselves?

_____

_____

_____

_____

_____

When we humble ourselves before God, we acknowledge not only that He is greater than us but also that we need Him to sustain us. We can accomplish some great things, yes; but God is the ultimate source of sustenance. By our submission and obedience to God, we invite Him to use His power to shape us as He pleases so that we can do those great things.

Take a minute to thank God that He never forces you to grow but gently guides you. And tell God that you want to obey Him no matter what, no matter when and no matter where.

4—DEPEND ON THE POTTER

Read 2 Corinthians 4 (yes, the whole chapter). We are merely weak human beings ("jars of clay," verse 7), but what treasure do we contain, and why should we never feel hopeless, alone or ruined (see verses 7-12)?

_____

_____

_____

_____

_____

No matter what happens in life, what have we been promised (see verses 15-18)?

_____

_____

_____

_____

What can you do daily to show that you are always connected to the One who sustains you?

_____

_____

_____

_____

Take a minute to thank God that no matter what you go through, you always have hope and you can depend on Jesus to always be with you, giving you whatever you need.

ENDNOTES

Session 6: Ultimate Courage
1. "San Francisco Earthquake History 1769-1879," *The Virtual Museum of the City of San Francisco*, 1995-2012. http://www.sfmuseum.org/alm/quakes1.html (accessed December 2012).
2. Ibid.
3. Ibid.
4. Ibid.

Session 7: Ultimate Encouragement
1. "Lexicon Results-Strong's G1410-dynamai," *The Blue Letter Bible*. http://www.blueletterbible.org/lang/lexicon/lexicon.cfm?strongs=G1410 (accessed January 2013).
2. *Greek Dictionary*, s.v. "hypophero," *Teknia*, 1995-2012. http://www.teknia.com/greek-dictionary/hypophero (accessed January 2013).

Session 9: Ultimate Redemption
1. Teddy Blue Abbott, "Cowboys," *The West*, Episode 5, The West Film Project and WETA, 2001. http://www.pbs.org/weta/thewest/program/episodes/five/cowboys.htm (accessed January 2012).
2. "Songs of the Plains—A Selection of Cowboy Folk Songs," *Archives of the West 1868-1874*, The West Film Project and WETA, 2001. http://www.pbs.org/weta/thewest/resources/five/songs.htm (accessed January 2012).
3. "Western Music (North America)," *Wikipedia, The Free Encyclopedia*, November 25, 2012. http://en.wikipedia.org/wiki/Western_music_(North_America) (accessed January 2012).

Session 10: Ultimate Allegiance
1. "Cowboy," *Wikipedia, The Free Encyclodedia*, December 27, 2012. http://en.wikipedia.org/wiki/Cowboy#Florida_Cowhunter_or_.22Cracker cowboy.22 (accessed January 2013).

Session 12: Ultimate Sustenance
1. Gary Speer, "Cowboys Knew Who the Real Boss Was on Trail Drives: The Cook," Life in the Old West. http://www.lifeintheoldwest.com/cowboys-knew-who-the-real-boss-was-on-trail-drives-the-cook/#more-2028.

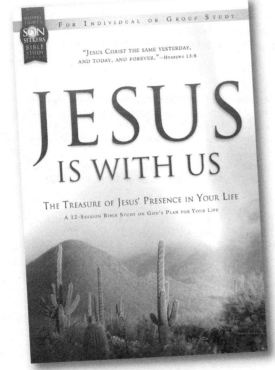